DEGREE OF LEVERAGE

DEGREE OF LEVERAGE: EMPIRICAL ANALYSIS FROM THE INSURANCE SECTOR

Samuel Gameli Gadzo

Copyright © 2018 by Samuel Gameli Gadzo.

ISBN:	Softcover	978-1-9845-6470-2
	eBook	978-1-9845-6469-6

All rights reserved. No part of this book may be reproduced or transmitted in any form or by any means, electronic or mechanical, including photocopying, recording, or by any information storage and retrieval system, without permission in writing from the copyright owner.

The views expressed in this work are solely those of the author and do not necessarily reflect the views of the publisher, and the publisher hereby disclaims any responsibility for them.

Any people depicted in stock imagery provided by Getty Images are models, and such images are being used for illustrative purposes only.
Certain stock imagery © Getty Images.

Print information available on the last page.

Rev. date: 11/05/2018

To order additional copies of this book, contact:
Xlibris
1-888-795-4274
www.Xlibris.com
Orders@Xlibris.com
787910

DEDICATION

To my wife Mrs Pamela Gadzo Daughter Mariam Seyram Gadzo

ACKNOWLEDGEMENTS

Those who contributed in diverse ways toward the production of this particular book merit more than acknowledgement for their constant encouragement without which the likelihood of giving up the task was very high. Special thanks go to my principal supervisor Dr. Emmanuel Ekow Asmah for his understanding, encouragement, and invaluable guidance when he was contact to help finalize this book. The completion of this book would not have been possible without his direction and mentoring. Thank you for your unflinching support and encouragement. I am greatly indebted to Professor John Gartchie Gatsi my mentor and senior brother for his timely counsel, motivation and the help he gave when structuring the title of the book. My gratitude goes to Mr Isaac Afful of the English Department of English at University of Ghana for editing the entire work.

I also acknowledge the authors whose names appear in the references and from whose work I have quoted. I wish to thank professional friends and family especially Holy Kportorgbi; Wisdom Kpano, Agormor Fafa, Micheal Mawulolo Gadzo, Valantina Serlorm Gadzo, Fafali Gadzo, Enyonam Gadzo, Selasie Gadzo; Selassie Aheto; Samuel Ayittah. My Father and Mother, Edward Oklu Gadzo and Mariam Boakyewaa Gadzo for their advice and constant motivation to finish this manuscript. Any limitations in this book, however, are exclusively mine. But the good comments must be shared among those named above.

TABLE OF CONTENTS

DEDICATION v
ACKNOWLEDGEMENTS vii
PREFACE xiii

CHAPTER ONE
INTRODUCTION TO DEGREE OF LEVERAGE 1
   1.0 Introduction 1
   1.1 Motivation for the study 4
   1.2 Purpose and objectives for the Study 6
   1.3 Hypotheses for the study 7
   1.4 Scope of the study 8
   1.5 Significance of the study 8
   1.6 Limitations and Delimitations of the study 9

CHAPTER TWO
OVERVIEW OF THE INSURANCE SECTOR OF GHANA AND THEORETICAL DEFINITION OF LEVERAGE 11
   2.0 Introduction 11
   2.1 Overview of the insurance sector of Ghana 12
   2.2 Theoretical definition of leverage 13

CHAPTER THREE
THEORETICAL FRAMEWORK OF LEVERAGE 16
   3.0 Introduction 16
   3.1 Irrelevance Modigliani and Miller theory 17

    3.1.1 M and M Proposition I 17
    3.1.2 M & M proposition II 18
  3.2 The Pecking Order Theory 19
    3.2.1 Implications of the pecking order theory 21
  3.3 The Static Trade-off Theory 21
    3.3.1 Implications of the static trade-off theory 22
    3.3.2 Bankruptcy Cost 23
  3.4 Free cash flow theory 24

CHAPTER FOUR
REVIEW OF MEASURES OF FINANCIAL
PERFORMANCE AND FIRM CHARACTERISTICS 26
  4.0 Introduction 26
  4.1 Financial performance measures 26
  4.2 Firm level characteristics 28
    4.2.1 Firm size 28
    4.2.2 Firm Age 30
    4.2.3 Firm Growth 30
  4.3 Macroeconomic variables 31
    4.3.1 Inflation Rate 31
    4.3.2 Gross Domestic Product (GDP) 32
    4.3.3 Exchange Rate 32

CHAPTER FIVE
EMPIRICAL REVIEW OF FINANCIAL
PERFORMANCE AND LEVERAGE OF FIRMS 34
  5.0 Introduction 34
  5.1 Relationship between financial performance and the
      degree of leverage of firms 35
  5.2 Analytical Framework 43

CHAPTER SIX
RESEARCH METHODS 46
  6.0 Introduction 46
  6.1 Research Design 46

6.2 Population for the study 48
6.3 Sampling and Sampling Procedure 48
6.4 Data collection Procedure 49
6.5 Measurement of variables 49
      6.5.1 Dependent variables 50
      6.5.2 The Independent Variables 51
      6.5.3 Firm Specific Variables 53
      6.5.4 Macroeconomic indicators 54
6.6 Panel regression model 55
6.7 Model specification for firm specific variable's 55
6.8 Model specification for macroeconomic variable's 56
6.9 Estimation method 56
6.10 Data preparation and analysis plan 58
6.11 Summary 58

CHAPTER SEVEN
NATURE OF DEGREE OF LEVERAGE AMONG
INSURANCE COMPANIES IN GHANA 59
7.1 Introduction 59
7.2 Descriptive statistics 60
7.3 Nature of degree of leverage 62

CHAPTER EIGHT
CORRELATION AND UNIT ROOT TEST ANALYSIS
OF THE VARIABLES 71
8.0 Introduction 71
8.1 Correlation analysis 72
8.2 Unit root analysis 77
8.3 The Hausman specification test 78

CHAPTER NINE
REGRESSION RESULTS AND DISCUSSION 80
9.1 Panel regression results 80
9.2 Regression for Performance Variables and
      Macroeconomic indicators 89

    9.3 Research hypothesis testing 91
        9.3.1 Hypothesis formulated for the degree of
            leverage variables 92
        9.3.2 Hypothesis formulated for the macroeconomic 93
        9.3.3 Hypothesis formulated for the firm specific
            variables.. 95

CHAPTER TEN
SUMMARY, CONCLUSION AND RECOMMENDATIONS.98
    10.1 Introduction 98
    10.2 Summary 99
    10.3 Conclusions 103
    10.4 Recommendations 104

REFERENCES 107
APPENDICES 115

PREFACE

The general objective of this book is to establish the relationship between capital structure and financial performance of insurance companies in Ghana. This study was prompted by the downward trend of the financial performance coupled with the less than one percent penetration rate of the insurance sector as was noted in the Ghana National Insurance Commission Report. The descriptive-causal research design was employed in the study and the panel regression model was used in the regression analysis. The sample for the study comprised 18 insurance companies from 2002 to 2017. The analysis and discussion of the data point to three key findings. First, the study revealed that greater proportion of the capital of insurance companies in Ghana is debt capital. The study also indicated significant differences between the financial performance indicators and capital structure of insurance companies with average age below and above twenty during the period under study. Using various measures of financial performance, the results indicated that capital structure exercises partial influence over financial performance. The results revealed that capital structure negatively affected financial performance of insurance companies in Ghana. The study therefore recommends that insurance companies should therefore consider increasing equity in their capital structure through capital raising ventures like private placement of shares so as to reduce the over reliance on debt. This will help in reducing the cost of debt thereby enhancing profitability.

CHAPTER ONE

INTRODUCTION TO DEGREE OF LEVERAGE

Learning Objectives

By the end of this chapter, you should:

- *have a better degree of leverage*
- *understand the motivation for conducting a study in leverage of insurance companies*
- *be able to comprehend the purpose and objectives for the study*
- *be able to enumerate the hypothesis for the study*
- *be able to comprehend the significance of the study*

1.0 Introduction

The degree of leverage of companies has been a major finance issue in academic circles as well as in the corporate world. Studies on degree of leverage have developed since the publication of the works of Modigliani and Millar (1958), which argued that despite the fact that the firm has debt or not, the overall value of the firm remains unchanged and that the shareholder's wealth cannot be enhanced by altering the debts into equity ratios. Abor (2008) in his contribution to the subject matter indicated that, degree of leverage decisions are crucial for any business organisation that aims at maximising the wealth of its shareholders and other stakeholders of the organisation.

The central focus of the topic is the size of equity capital and debt that should be increased in order to achieve the objectives of the institution to maximise the financial performance of the company (Dhanasekaran, Kumar, Sandhya & Saravanan, 2012). Most recent studies have confirmed the existence of a relationship between the value of the company's degree of leverage, which means that the change in the degree of leverage of the companies affects the financial performance of the business and the value of the company.

The major theories of the degree of leverage issues have also recognized the benefits of financial leverage in firm financing while avoiding the cost of financial distress. For the purpose of the current study three dominant theoretical models within which other theories are embedded are reviewed and infused in the model of the study. These are the static trade-off model, the pecking order model and the free cash flow theory. The static trade-off theory according to Ross, Westerfield, Jeff and Jordan (2011), indicates that firms borrow up to the point where the tax benefit from an extra dollar in debt is exactly equal to the cost that comes from the increased profitability of financial distress.

The pecking order theory concluded that the total amount of debt in the degree of leverage of companies will reflect the firms' cumulative need for external funds. The free cash flow theory on the other hand expatiated that extremely high debt levels would increase firm value despite the threat of finance distress when a firms' operating cash flow significantly surpasses its profitable investment opportunities (Naizuli, 2011). The influence of these theories on the current study has been accessed to validate their impact on financial performance of the insurance companies.

Financial performance is a slanted measure of how well an organisation can use the assets in their possession to generate revenues for the core purpose for which it was established. Gatsi

(2012) posits that financial performance measures like profitability and liquidity, among others, provide a valuable tool to interest groups to evaluate the past financial performance and the current position of a firm. These ratios can be classified into two main types, namely profitability ratios in relation to sales and profitability ratios in relation to investment.

Ishfaq, Naveed and Zulfquar (2010) opine that, degree of leverage differs from one industry to the other and that it is relevant to distinguish the degree of leverage of insurance companies from other companies. This is because these companies expect funds to settle the claims or pay damages at the time of loss. From this backdrop, Ahmad, Naveed, and Zulfquar (2011), acknowledged that the current business environment is unsustainable without insurance companies because of the risky nature of the modern business environment coupled with the fact that, the corporate firms have limited capacity to mitigate all risks that they face during their operations.

The basic theory of insurance is capitalised on the insurer spreading its risk over many clients, where some of them will sustain losses and make claims, but most of them will not. The insurer bears only part of the risk, while the other part is born by the insured in the form of surfeit on the insurance policy. To deal with correlated-risk insurance, Cheng, et al (2009) opined that insurers use an insurance pooling technique, where many insurance companies work in cooperation by joining their capital and sharing the risks.

From the backdrop of risk sharing, it is important for the insurance sectors in developing countries such as Ghana to better understand the influence that the nature of their funding sources has on their performance. Again, it is important to provide insurance companies with knowledge that relates to the nature of their degree of leverage. This would assist financial managers to perk up their financing decisions regarding their financing mix. By taking into account some key variables that influence their degree of leverage, financial managers of insurance companies can better achieve their overall performance goals.

1.1 Motivation for the study

The persistent poor financial performance of the insurance companies in Ghana has become a great concern among researchers and practitioners. The National Insurance Commission's Report (2017), revealed a decline in the major financial performance indicators of the sector with an industry average of return on asset recording 9%, 6 %, 5 %, 3%, 3%, 7%, 6%-1%, 0.04% and 0.03% for 2008, 2009, 2010, 2011, 2012, 2013, 2014, 2015, 2016 and 2017 respectively as depicted in Figure 1.1.

Table 1.1 Trend of ROA

Source: National Insurance Commission's Report (2017)

while return on equity recorded was 23%, 21 %, 20.23 %,20,1 %,18 %, 20%, 18% 17%, 6% and 5.16% for 2008, 2009, 2010, 2011, 2012, 2013, 2014, 2015, 2016 and 2017 as depicted in figure 1.2.

Figure 1.2: Trend of Return on Equity

Source: National Insurance Commission's Report (2017)

The trend indicates a decline of about 30 percent in the financial indicators year on year. Moreover, in terms of the penetration rate, the industry recorded less than 2 percent penetration rate. This means that the insurance companies in Ghana have not done enough in trying to encourage majority of Ghanaians to have an insurance policy.

The statistics above shows a decline in the performance of the insurance companies, but could degree of leverage which has been described by Dhanasekaran, Kumar, Sandhya and Saravanan (2012, p. 6), as "the blood of any business" be the cause of this decline? Arising from the findings of Najjar and Petrov (2011), Ahmad et al. (2011) and Dhanasekaran, et al (2012) that the degree of leverage employed by insurance companies could influence their financial performance, then there is the need for a study to be conducted on the degree of leverage of the insurance companies in Ghana to demystify what causes the decline in their financial performance indicators.

It is on this basis that the present researcher was propelled to investigate whether insurance companies in Ghana have debt as a component of their capital mix and if so, what influence their degree of leverage has on their financial performance. Furthermore, previous studies on degree of leverage and profitability has been centred on listed institutions of which insurance companies constitute less than one percent of the entire population hence those studies did not reveal the actual situation in relation to insurance companies. Apart from the above issues, studies on degree of leverage and firm performance has failed to incorporate the effect of macroeconomic factors on the performance of companies especially in the case of Africa where macroeconomic factors continually fluctuate to the disadvantage of profit making organisations.

The current study is conducted to fill the research gap by investigating the relationship between the degree of leverage and the financial performance of insurance firms in Ghana in other to provide an insight for managers and stakeholders to enhance their decision making when it comes to issues of degree of leverage. Also the outcome of the study provides literature on the effect of macroeconomic variables on firm performance as well as the introduction of how the free cash flow theory can be applied to the degree of leverage of insurance companies in Ghana.

1.2 Purpose and objectives for the Study

Every company operate with a fund which might come from debt or equity source, these funds are then used for the operational activities of the company to generate profit. This implies that when the firm is not able to generate profit, their source of finance can be a major cause of it. If that is anything to go by, then the study investigated the relationship between degree of leverage and financial performance of insurance companies in Ghana.

The main objective of the study was to examine the degree of leverage and its effect on the financial performance of insurance companies in Ghana.

The following specific objectives guided the study:

1. Determine the degree of leverage being practised by insurance firms in Ghana.
2. Test the relationship between degree of leverage ratios and financial performance of insurance companies in Ghana.
3. Determine whether macroeconomic variables influence the financial performance of insurance companies in Ghana.
4. Establish a relationship between financial performance ratios and firm specific factors of the insurance companies in Ghana.

1.3 Hypotheses for the study

The following hypotheses guided the study:

Testable hypotheses

H1: Financial performance has a relationship with short–term debt ratio of insurance companies in Ghana.
H2: Financial performance has a relationship with long–term debt ratio of insurance companies in Ghana.
H3: Financial performance has a relationship with total debt ratio of insurance companies in Ghana.
H4: Financial performance of insurance companies in Ghana has a relationship with inflation rate
H5: Financial performance of insurance companies in Ghana has a relationship with gross domestic product.
H6: Financial performance of insurance companies in Ghana has a relationship with exchange rate.
H7: Financial performance of insurance companies in Ghana has a relationship with their size.
H8: Financial performance of insurance companies in Ghana has a relationship with their premium growth.
H9: Financial performance of insurance companies in Ghana has a relationship with their age.

1.4 Scope of the study

Degree of leverage is broad but the scope for the purpose of the current studies is based on short term debt, long term debt and the total debt. The reason for this scope is derived from studies such as Head and Watson (2010), Ross, Westerfield, Jeff and Jordan (2011) ; Ahmad, Naveed and Zulfqar (2011) which indicated that the above listed scope fully explains the issues of degree of leverage. In relation to geographical scope, the study places emphasis on all general insurance companies that are incorporated under the Ghana Companies Code 1963 Act 179 and have prepared their financial statements covering the period from 2002 to 2017. The reason for not considering life insurance companies is because of the division of life insurance business from general businesses as stipulated by the National Insurance commission of Ghana in 2017.

1.5 Significance of the study

The financial performance of any firm as stated by Ahmad, Naveed and Zulfqar (2011) does not only play the role of increasing the market value of that specific firm but it impacts significantly on the growth of the whole industry. Consequently this influences the overall prosperity of the economy. Conducting research on the financial performance of insurers is of importance in the corporate finance literature because as intermediaries, these institutions do not only provide the mechanism of risk transfer but also they help to channel the funds in what may be regarded as an appropriate way to support the business activities in the economy.

It is in this regard that Amartey – Vondee (2007) made mention of the fact that, insurance companies are important to both the businesses and individuals as they indemnify the losses and put them in the same positions as they were before the occurrence of the loss. In addition, Ahmad *et al.* (2011) added that, insurers provide economic and social benefits in the society that is through the prevention of losses, reduction in anxiousness, and by increasing employment.

Therefore, the current business world without insurance companies is unsustainable because risky businesses do not have the capacity to retain all types of risk in the extremely uncertain environment.

For the academic world, this study sheds more light on the issue of degree of leverage which has much been discussed since the publication of the prepositions by (Modiglani & Miller, 1958). The study further adds to existing literature on insurance and serve as an impetus for further research.

For practitioners, the study is relevant and of much interest to financial controllers, finance managers and managing directors particularly those working in the insurance firms as it provides insight into how to finance the operations of insurance companies. In addition, the study may be useful to practitioners who would want to obtain an idea as to whether degree of leverage has an effect on insurance firm's profitability. As such, the researcher believes that there is the need to fill an important gap in understanding degree of leverage decisions for insurance companies in the developing world. Considering these points, this study in no small way is of immerse significance.

1.6 Limitations and Delimitations of the study

The study was restricted to only insurance companies which had their financial statements with the National Insurance Commission covering the period of 2002 to 2017. Banking and non-financial institutions were also not considered in the study. As a result, the findings are only limited to the insurance sector because of how issues involving insurance companies have been understudied over the years in Ghana. The study was also restricted to only secondary sources of data. The use of the financial data, the computation of financial performance and leverage ratios of 18 insurance companies were not sufficient as the data point should have covered about thirty companies. It was also difficult tracing most insurance companies' financial statement. This results from the constant mergers and the acquisition and change on company names which has engulfed the insurance industry for the past decade. The number of years was increased to cater for the relatively small number of insurance companies involved in the study. Also to effectively trace the companies for changes in their names, the researcher personally visited the companies to request for their previously registered names before reconciling those names with this current ones found with the National Insurance Commission.

CHAPTER TWO

OVERVIEW OF THE INSURANCE SECTOR OF GHANA AND THEORETICAL DEFINITION OF LEVERAGE

Learning Objectives

By the end of this chapter, you should be able to;

- *comprehend the structure of the Ghanaian insurance sector*
- *understand the theoretical definition of leverage*

2.0 Introduction

The review of literature is in four main parts: the overview of the insurance industry in Ghana; the theoretical review, empirical review and conceptual framework. The theoretical review presents perspectives on propositions and ideas of some earlier researchers, authors and educators on the theories of degree of leverage and financial performance measures. Under the empirical review, the research methodology, findings and recommendations of some researchers in relation to degree of leverage and financial performance are reviewed.

2.1 Overview of the insurance sector of Ghana

The Ghanaian insurance industry is categorised under the services sector of the economy of Ghana. The service sector is one of the most important sectors and has shown significant development over the past decade. In 2011, the sector contributed about 35 percent of Ghana's total Gross Domestic Product and produced the highest growth rate of 10.3 percent among other sectors (All Africa Global Media, 2017). The insurance industry in Ghana is managed by the National Insurance Commission which has been given the mandate by an act of Parliament to play this oversight role.

The National Insurance Commission was established under Insurance Law 1989 (PNDC Law 227), but now operate under the Insurance Act, 2006 (Act 724). The major objective of the NIC, as outlined in Act 724, is to guarantee effective administration, regulation and manage the business of insurance in Ghana. The NIC is mandated to carry out a wide range of functions including licensing of entities, setting of standards and setting of codes for practitioners. The Commission is also mandated to approve rates of insurance premiums and commissions, provide a bureau for the resolution of complaints and arbitrate insurance claims when disputes arise.

The insurance industry in Ghana has contributed immensely to the growth of the financial services sector and helped drive the economy of Ghana for the past years. The insurance market is becoming more vibrant and continues to make progress especially the period between 2002 and 2011. This was confirmed by the NIC report (2017, p.5), as it was reported that "There was a general increase in premium income for both classes of business from GH¢ 92.5 million in 2004 to nearly GH¢ 628.5 million in 2011. Both the life and the non-life recorded a growth rate of 37.2 percent between 2010 and 2011. The contributions of Total Gross Premium to the GDP still remain at 1 percent".

The industry has a huge potential, which has barely been scratched. Prospects in both Life and Non-life businesses are yet to be fully tapped and the petro-chemical industry is rife with recent oil discovery in commercial quantities. For insurance companies to get these prospects on board and strategically position themselves for effective delivery of services, it is critical for them to make information in all facets of insurance industry available for public use (NIC Report, 2011).

Competition in the industry has also made statistics more relevant and influential in decision-making. As stated, global trends indicate that knowledge-based societies are developing faster than those who lack the opportunity to access relevant information on issues affecting their lives. Information therefore, has become a powerful tool in modern development, and insurance companies would have to ensure constant flow of detail information about their operations to the public in order to build confidence in the clients, prospects and potential investors.

2.2 Theoretical definition of leverage

This section discusses the views of authorities on degree of leverage, theories of degree of leverage and financial performance. The term degree of leverage is a widely known terms in the finance world, many scholars have given their own views about its definitions since the earlier work of Modigliani and Miller (1958). Some of these definitions are reviewed below;

Degree of leverage is the specific mix of debt and equity that a firm uses to finance its operations (Abor, 2008). This brief definition lends itself for review considering the fact that it placed emphasis on specific proportion of debt and equity used for financing organisations. Abor (2008), then added that, the concept is actually a mixture of different securities and that a firm can choose among many alternative sources of capital such as the issue of large amount of debt or very little debt; arrangement of lease financing; use warrants; issue convertible bonds; sign forward contracts or trade bond swaps;

and issue of dozen of distinct securities in countless combinations. In summary, the definition provided by Abor (2008) did not consider the fact that the sources of capital could occur from time horizons.

In relation to the definition provided by Abor, (2008), Ishfaq Naveed and Zulfqar (2010), recognised its flaws and defined the degree of leverage concept as the relationship between the various forms of finance; thus, long term and short term sources making mention of debentures, bonds, bank and trade credits, commercial papers, preference share capital and equity capital. The writers further added that, the term then signifies the relationship between equity and debt capital that are ascertain in a target proportion to attain the objectives of the firm. Ishfaq *et al.* (2010) provided a clear understanding of the concept but they did not clearly explain the proportion prepositions of the degree of leverage concept.

Also, Ross, Westerfield, Jeff and Jordan, (2011) provided a definition which relates to the proportion prepositions by defining the term as the proportion of a firm's finance from current liabilities, long – term debt and equity. Ross et al (2011) also indicated that degree of leverage is a firm's choice of how much debt it should have relative to equity and they presented the pie model which considered the value of the firm finance as a pie which can be divided among the various providers of funds. The authors further indicated that such a choice is a strategic one which has many implications for the firm and for that matter degree of leverage should be a matter of policy by the directors in order to serve the ultimate interest of the shareholder and other stakeholders of the company.

To add to literature on the subject matter, Saad (2010) opined that degree of leverage basically means the manner in which a firm finance its assets through the combination of equity, debt, or hybrid of securities. The present researcher views this definition as a contemporary one which could not just highlight the proportion issue, but it has also added a new dimension of a hybrid security been part of the fray. Abu-Rub (2012) therefore indicated that the firm can issue different securities in countless combinations but it attempts to find the particular combinations that maximize market value and will also lend itself to a lower cost.

From the plethora of definitions, the researcher considers degree of leverage from a triangular perspective to mean a situation that consist of the proportion of finance the company receives from both short and long term debt, equity and hybrid capital. Several theories have been developed to analyse alternative degree of leverage and explained by academic scholars and researchers in corporate finance. These include the irrelevance optimal capital theory of (Modigliani and Miller 1958). This has come to stay as the "M& M theory"

CHAPTER THREE

THEORETICAL FRAMEWORK OF LEVERAGE

Learning Objectives

After studying this chapter, you will be able to:

- *Modigliani and Miller theory 1*
- *Modigliani and Miller theory 2*
- *Pecking order theory*
- *Static trade-off theory*
- *Free cashflow theory*

3.0 Introduction

Several theories have been developed to analyse alternative degree of leverage and explained by academic scholars and researchers in corporate finance. These include the irrelevance optimal capital theory of (Modigliani and Miller 1958). This has come to stay as the "M& M theory"

3.1 Irrelevance Modigliani and Miller theory

Modigliani and Miller (1958) cannot be left out when the discussion of degree of leverage is in force. In corporate finance literature, these two scholars are credited as the originators of the degree of leverage theories. In their contribution to theories on degree of leverage, they came out with two main propositions namely M and M proposition I and M and M proposition II.

3.1.1 M and M Proposition I

The first preposition put forward by Modigliani and Miller (1958), states that a firms cost of capital which is represented by a weighted average cost of capital remains stable at all levels of leverage. The import of this is that, there is no optimal degree of leverage for a particular company and for that matter, an industry. Their notion was that, it is completely irrelevant how a firm chooses to arrange its finance. In other words, the value of the firm is independent of its degree of leverage. In drawing this conclusion, the following assumptions were made; an individual can borrow at the same rate and conditions as corporations, such that if individuals can borrow at a higher rate, one can easily show that corporations can increase firm value by borrowing.

Secondly, that the capital markets were perfect assumption was central to their discussion and it meant that, bankruptcy risk could be ignored so that distressed companies could always raise additional finance in a perfect market. The notion of the perfect capital market is given the meaning that; the stocks of different companies are homogenous and they can serve as perfect substitute, Investors a consensus about the expected future returns for all shares and all securities are traded under perfect market conditions. In sum according to the theory, the way in which a firm arrange its assets can have no impact on the value of the firm. The value of a firm is derived from the net present value of investments the firm has committed its current resources into.

3.1.2 M & M proposition II

Modigliani and Miller (1963) amended their model in their second paper and the result was the proposition II. The amendment according to Kayo and Limura (2010) was done in relation to their acknowledgement of the existence of corporate tax and the tax deductibility of interest payment. This means that as the firm increases its leverage, by replacing equity with debt, it shields more and more of its profits from tax. However they indicated that, although varying degree of leverage of the firm may not change the firms' total value; it does cause important changes in the firms' debt and equity.

M&M II demonstrated that, as the firm raises its gearing proportion, the increase in leverage raises the risk of the equity and therefore the required return, or cost of equity. Modigliani and Miller (1963), Proposition II indicated that the cost of equity depends on three things: the required rate of return on the firm's assets; the firm's cost of debts and the firm's debt-equity ratio. Modigliani and Miller (1963), proposition II therefore states that, a firm's cost of equity capital has a positive linear relationship with its degree of leverage. Modigliani and Miller therefore concluded that the cost of capital or the required rate on return on the firm's assets does not depend on the debt-equity ratio; it is the same no matter what the debt-equity ratio is. The import of this is that the firm's overall cost of capital is unaffected by its degree of leverage.

Hence, the fact that the cost of debt is lower than the cost of equity means that, the benefit of cheaper debt capital is exactly offset by the increase in the cost of equity from borrowing as a result of the increment in financial risk exposed to the equity holders of the company. In other words, the change in the weight of debts and equity in the degree of leverage of a particular firm is exactly offset by the change in the cost of equity, so the cost of capital of the company stays the same. Modigliani and Miller having proved the irrelevance theory of degree of leverage, has left the finance world into what the researcher can describe as the degree of leverage puzzle since the arguments put forward by other scholars on the relevancy of the term has been found to be the reality after proving that the assumptions put forward by those great scholars does not hold in the real world. It is in the face of this that, other theories have also sprung up in corporate finance over the years.

Gatsi (2012), recognised that, the fundamental theoretical model of degree of leverage centres on some key assumptions which include; the idea that firms have information that investors do not have, and that the interest of managers, equity – holders and debt holders may not coincide. The researcher also found that though the theories have also recognized the benefits of financial leverage in firm financing while avoiding friction and bankruptcy costs of financial distress arises the need to review friction and bankruptcy cost. These recognitions have led to three dominating theoretical models, namely the Static Trade – Off model, the pecking order theory and the free cash flow theories. Enshrined in these three theories are additional ones but the for the purpose of the current study, the three theories and some of their accompanying theories are used to explain the degree of leverage decisions of insurance companies in Ghana. The bankruptcy cost is considered in terms of the static trade – off choice while the information asymmetry, market timing theory and signalling theory, as noted by Abu-Rub (2012), are rooted in the pecking order theory frame work.

3.2 The Pecking Order Theory

The theory according to Heng and Ong (2011) explains how a firm can use internally generated funds to initially finance their operations instead of external borrowings. The initial explanation of the theory according to the researchers, involves issue costs and the ease with which source of finance are accessed. Graham and Leary (2010) noted that according to the pecking order theory firms do not have a well defined target debt to equity ratio and each firm's observed debt ratio simply reflects the firm's cumulative requirement for external finance over an extended period. In a related literature, Akoto and Gatsi (2010) stating their opinion on the model, argued that raising external finance is costly because insiders have more information about the firms' prospects than outside investors, and outside investors know this and would thus demand higher returns on their investments. From this point of view of outside investors, equity is riskier than debt and therefore demands a higher result premium for equity than for debt. Thus, insiders perceive debt to be a better source of funding than equity, and internal funding is even better.

Kayo and Limura (2010), discovered that transaction cost may be a significant determinant of degree of leverage choice; this reflected in the short term debt ratios which are negatively related to firm size. This view was supported by Leary and Roberts (2010), were of the view that although the fundamental basis of the pecking order theory is on adverse selection, based on information asymmetry, it is not necessary for information asymmetry to exist for a financing hierarchy to arise, other factors such as the expensive of issuing various classes of securities and incentive conflicts can create their own order for capital.

Levy and Post (2005), therefore opined that firms prefer retained earnings to debt and would only issue equity as a last resort. Abor and Biekpe (2009) supported this by saying that debt financing will only be used when there is an inadequate amount of internal funding available, and equity will only be used as a last resort. However, El-Wahid and Singapurwoko (2011), were of the opinion that even if pecking order exists, companies may at times choose to ignore it in order to maintain a spare debt capacity or to retain internal funding in favour of debt if they believe that it will be required to fund attractive future investment opportunities. In support of this Erol (2011), stated that the reason that companies may choose to maintain spare debt capacity is to maintain their credit rating since it can take several years to recover from a downgrade. Retain internal funding in favour of debt improves the company's ability to withstand a period of poor performance and allows it to execute a recovery plan

3.2.1 Implications of the pecking order theory

Barclay and Clifford (2005) indicated that companies that identify small investment opportunities and substantial free cash flow will have low or even negative debt ratios because the cash will be used to settle the debt. It therefore suggests that firms with high-growth prospects with lower operating cash flow will have high debt ratios because of their reluctance to raise new equity. It should be emphasised that where information asymmetry does not clearly manifests itself, the firm will then turn to debt if additional funds are needed, and eventually issue equity to cover any remaining capital requirements. It is clear at this point that, firms would prefer internal sources to costly external finance (Gatsi, 2012).Thus, import of the pecking order theory is that, firms that are profitable and therefore generate high earnings are expected to use less debt capital than those that do not generate high earnings.

3.3 The Static Trade-off Theory

Frydenberg (2004) explained that, the theory explains how a firm's optimal debt ratio is determined by a trade-off between the benefits and obligations of borrowing, holding the firm's assets and investment plans constant. The firm can use debt in place of equity, or equity for debt until the firm ultimately maximised the value of the firm. The benefit of debt according to Frydenberg (2004) is primarily the tax-shield effect, which emanates from the fact that interest on debt is deductible on the profit and loss account.

The costs of debt is directly and indirectly associated to bankruptcy costs such that as the firm increase it's gearing level the inability to pay the obligations attached to the debt also increases enhancing the probability of bankruptcy of firm. In the more general trade-off theory several other arguments are used for why firms might try to adjust their degree of leverage to some target. Leverage also depends on restrictive covenants in the debt-contracts, takeover possibilities and the reputation of management. In view of this,

Graham and Leary (2010) proposed a negative correlation between debt and monitoring costs.

The theory according to Ross, Westerfield, Jeff and Jordan (2011), states that firms borrow up to the point where the tax benefit from an extra dollar in debt is exactly equal to the cost that comes from the increased profitability of financial distress. Ross *et al* (2011) further noted that the static theory is called static theory because it assumes that the firm is fixed in terms of its assets and operations and it only considers possible changes in the debt – equity ratio. They also stated that the model is not capable of identifying a precise optimal degree of leverage, but it does point out two of the more relevant factors, namely taxes and financial distress.

The trade-off theory indicates the exposure of the firm to bankruptcy and agency cost against tax benefits associated with debt use. Bankruptcy cost is a cost directly incurred when the perceived probability that the firm will default on financing is greater than zero. One of the bankruptcy costs is liquidation cost, which represents the loss of value as a result of liquidating the net assets of the firm. Another bankruptcy cost is distress cost, which is the cost a firm incurs if stakeholders believe that the firm will discontinue. The static trade – off theory has been criticised by many authors, including Miller (1977), who argued that the static trade – off model implies that firms should be highly leveraged than they really are, as the tax savings of debt seem large while the costs of financial distress seem minor.

3.3.1 Implications of the static trade-off theory

The tax benefit from leverage include; the use of debt as a factor of the ownership structure that disciplines manager; debt is a useful signalling tool that is used to inform the investors about a message of the firms level of excellence and Debt also reduces the excessive consumption of perquisites because creditors demand annual payments on the outstanding loans (Ahmad *et al* 2011). Therefore, implies that debt is obviously important to the firms that are in a tax – paying position (Abor 2008). Because of this, firms with substantial accumulated losses will get less value from the interest tax shield (Abu-Rub 2012). Again, firms that have a sizeable amount of tax shields from other sources, such as depreciation, will get less benefit from leverage. It should further be noted that not all firms have the same tax rate. The higher the tax rate the greater the incentive to borrow (Ross *et al*, 2011).

The static trade-off model also implies that firms with a greater risk of experiencing financial distress will borrow less than firms with a lower risk of financial distress. For example, all things being equal the greater the volatility in earnings before interest and tax, the less a firm should borrow. It should also be noted that financial distress is more costly for some firms than for others. The cost of financial distress depends primarily on the firm's assets. In particular, financial distress costs will be determined by how easily ownership of those assets can be transferred.

3.3.2 Bankruptcy Cost

Bankruptcy cost are the costs incurred when the perceived probability that the firm will default on financing is greater than zero (Abor; 2008). Ross Westerfied, Jeff, and Jordan (2011) further explained that, bankruptcy cost means the cost that a firm incurs when a firm fails to honour its debts obligation and stands on the possibility of being closed down. According to them, the cost of bankruptcy may be both direct and indirect. Examples of direct bankruptcy costs are the legal and administrative costs in the bankruptcy process while the loss in profits incurred by the firm as a result of the unwillingness of stakeholders to do business with them is an example of indirect bankruptcy costs.

Saunders and Cornet (2004), mentioned that the direct costs are often small in relation to corporate market value whiles indirect costs are substantial. Levy and Post (2005) also added that customer dependency on a firm's goods and services and the high probability of bankruptcy affect the solvency of firms. Abor and Biekpe (2009,

p. 10) in their view on the subject matter, indicated that "if a business is perceived to be close to bankruptcy, customers may be less willing to buy its goods and services because of the risk that the firm may not be able to meet its warranty obligations" and further explained that employees might be less inclined to work for the business and suppliers are less likely to extend trade credit. Kim, Heshmati and Aoun (2006) stated that such restrictions or limitations can affect a firm's value and its performance, because it may eventually have to forge attractive investment opportunities leading to underinvestment. This could adversely impact on the profitability and existence of the firm.

Rauh and Sufi (2010) contend that firms may be unable to pay their debts if they over-borrow and become financially distressed. Nevertheless, it is reasonable for firms to increase value because of tax deductibility of debt. It should be noted that bankruptcy cost increases with increased debt use thus reducing the value of the firm (Saad, 2010). As a result, managers of financially distressed firms would advocate for less debt in their degree of leverage relative to their low-debt counterparts so as to safeguard against underinvestment and associated problems. In conclusion, Berk and DeMarzo (2011) posited that if bankruptcy is costly to managers, perhaps because they would lose benefits of control or reputation then debt finance should rather create incentives for managers to work harder, consume fewer prerequisites and make better investment decisions.

3.4 Free cash flow theory

Free cash flow refers to the amount of cash that a company has left over after it has paid all of its expenses, including investments (Afrasiabishani, Ahmadinia & Hesami, 2012). It is important in degree of leverage studies because it allows a company to pursue opportunities that enhance shareholder value. Without capital, it's tough to develop new products, make acquisitions, pay dividends and reduce debt (Afrasiabishani, et al, 2012). Related to degree of leverage this theory explains that mitigation of free cash flow by paying interest of debt and dividends prevent a manager from probable deviations to neglect the company's income for personal purposes. Because of law requirements, paying the principal and interest of debt is preferred to paying dividends to diminish the level of free cash flow (Afrasiabishani, Ahmadinia & Hesami, 2012).

CHAPTER FOUR

REVIEW OF MEASURES OF FINANCIAL PERFORMANCE AND FIRM CHARACTERISTICS

Learning Objective

After studying this chapter, the learner should be able to:

- *measures of financial performance*
- *access firm characteristics*

4.0 Introduction

The chapter cover issues relating to the empirical review of measures of financial performance and the empirical review of the characteristics of a firm.

4.1 Financial performance measures

Firm performance assessment has several dimensions. Performance measures could be financial or non-financial performance, market or accounting performance. The concept of financial performance is based on the comparison of the cash outflows required for implementing a premeditated alternative with the cash inflows that this alternative is expected to generate (Naizuli, 2011). Watson and Head (2010) suggested two broad measures of financial performance-absolute measure and relative measure. The absolute measure assesses performance based on the absolute quantum of profit. "Profit-equivalent" connotes varied forms of profit. One weakness of the absolute measure is its inability to relate the profit to the resources used to generate profit. Absolute measure may not provide quality information for performance comparison decisions.

Relative performance measures are much useful for inter and intra firm comparisons because they relate profit with resources used in generating such profits. Desai and Dharmapala (2007), Saad (2010) and several researchers used relative performance measures. Pervasive in literature is net profit margin (NPM), return on Equity (ROE), and return on assets (ROA). The appropriateness of each of the measures, according to Gupta and Newberry (1997), depends on the focus of the research in question. NPM has featured in most degree of leverage research. This can be explained by the fact that most of the researchers conduct the study by relating degree of leverage on statement of financial position items rather than on income statement item. Gadzo, Akoto & Gatsi (2014) chose ROA as performance measure over ROE because the latter does not capture the entirety of performance from both debt and equity perspective.

It is important to discuss the relationship between profit and ROA as well as how degree of leverage is likely to affect this relationship from a theoretical perspective. All things being equal, high profit should translate into high return on asset. This proposition is valid if increased profit is as a result of increase in efficiency level. Put differently, return on asset will only improve if the rate increase in profit is more than the rate of increase in degree of leverage used in generating profit. As discussed earlier, degree of leverage has the potential of affecting total income, hence affect the expenditure and ultimately, increase profit after interest and tax. It is expected that the effective and efficient use of capital available will reflect as higher ROA, ROE and NPM. This thinking is however, illusive if the capital sources trigger a disproportionate increase in capital used. For instance, it is possible to achieve increase in financial performance with the used of more retain earnings and not necessarily through acquisition of more debt capital.

It becomes imperative to juxtapose ROA, ROE and NPM –degree of leverage relationship with Gatsi, Gadzo, Anipa & Ameyibor (2016) observation that in contemporary times, management compensation is tied to effective use of capital at its disposal. If the self-interest seeking proposition of agency theory is something to go by, then it is possible for management to pursue after tax profit maximisation objective to the detriment of ROA. Indeed, this is where degree of leverage mechanisms play a role in the financial performance relationship. The dynamics of this role is what this research sought to establish.

4.2 Firm level characteristics

Firm level characteristics for the purpose of the current study are viewed as those traits that can be identified to a specific firm or industry. In view of literatures reviewed some of the firm level characteristics that influence the degree of leverage and financial performance include;

4.2.1 Firm size

Symeou (2008), indicated that, firm size influences the performance of most institutions, the study advances the understanding of the relationship between firm size and performance by examining whether firms enjoying higher growth potential are better performers. It builds on arguments presented in the literature on small economies to suggest that small economy size could contain firm growth potential and by extension firm performance. Abor and Beikpe (2005) and Abor (2008), emphasised that, firm size contributes to firms profitability and that large firms have greater chances of contracting more funds to finance their operations while small firms might not obtain the same funds. The effect of aged of institutions on their financial performance is not so different from their size because as the company grows all things being equal their size are also expected to increase hence their ability to increase operations which would facilitate improvement in their financial performance.

Sales growth is also significantly important in that from the degree of leverage theories reviewed such as pecking order theory, and information asymmetry, there is a relationship between financial performance and sales growth. Large firms are seen to be more diversified and therefore have lower difference in earnings which gives them an upper hand in tolerating high debt ratios (Ahmad *et al*, 2011). Smaller firms on the other hand may find it relatively more costly to decide. Thus lenders to larger firms are more likely to recover their funds than lenders to smaller firms. This simply means that larger firms will have higher debt. Empirical evidence on the relationship between size and degree of leverage supports a positive relationship.

Scholarly works as done by Barclay and Clifford, (2005), Al-Bashs and Sentic, (2008) suggest that smaller firms are likely to use equity finance while larger firms are likely to use debt. Cassar *et al.*, (2003), Esperanca *et al.*, (2003) and Hall, Hutchinson and Michaelas (2004) all found a positive relationship between firm size and long term debt ratios but a negative relationship between size and short term debt ratios. Graham (2000) after considering the size of the firm argued in his work that large scale companies which persistently earn high profit mostly operate with low debt levels indicating that they would rather retain their profit for both expansion and operational activities. However in the banking sector which belongs to the financial industry just as the insurance sector, Cassa and Holmes (2003) and Hall, *et al.* (2004) who all work on the banking industry established that a negative relationship between profitability and both long-term debt and short-term debt ratios.

4.2.2 Firm Age

As a firm continues in business, it establishes itself as a going concern thereby increasing its capacity to take on more debt. This therefore makes age positively related to debt. Age of the firm is a standard measure of reputation in degree of leverage models because as a firm continues longer in business, it establishes itself as a going concern and therefore increases its capacity to take on more debt making age positively related to debt. Asimakopoulos, *et al* (2009), indicated that a firm's profitability is positively affected by size, sales growth and investment. On the other hand, leverage and current assets negatively related with profitability. Hall et al., (2004) concurred to the above aspect of degree of leverage noting that age is positively related to long-term debt but negatively related to short-term debt. Esperanca et al., (2003), however, found that age is negatively related to both long-term and short-term debt. Green, (2002) also found that age has a negative influence on the probability of incurring debt in the initial capital equation, and no impact in the additional capital equation.

4.2.3 Firm Growth

Firm Growth is likely to place a greater demand on internally generated funds and push the firm into borrowing. Empirical evidence from studies conducted on sales growth and the dependent variables are quite varying with respect to conclusions. The nature of the relationship between firm growth potential and firm performance was examined by Kosmidou (2008) after employing stochastic frontier analysis on data for 54 incumbent telecommunications firms from an equal number of economies for the period 1990-2007.

Controlling for the effects of competition, firm governance structure, and institutional risk, inter alia, the findings suggest that firm growth potential is not necessarily a limiting factor as both firms in small and large economies can operate efficiently. Yet, higher growth potential is more important for firms operating in small than in large economies. By extension, firm growth potential is more important for small rather than large firms. Some researchers found positive relationship between firm growths and leverage (Gatsi, Gadzo, Opkoti & Anipa, 2015). Other evidence showed that higher growth firms use less debt, as such indicated negative relationship between growth and debt ratio (Dhanasekaran, *et al*, 2012).

4.3 Macroeconomic variables

In relation to the other macroeconomic control variables, such as GDP, inflations and exchange rates are important because the overall economic activities affect the insurance business. During the period of flourishing economic activity, demand on insurance companies decreases because the risk that companies faces reduced relatively to period of deteriorating macroeconomic indicators.

4.3.1 Inflation Rate

Inflation rate is the persistent increase in the general price level in a given economy over a given period of time. Studies relating to degree of leverage have found out that, the rate of inflation influences the degree of leverage and the financial performance of firms. Such studies include; Kosmidou (2008) found that the rate of inflation positively affect the monetary contraction for large firms but remain stable for small firms that rely on private debt and concluded that, inflation is significant in the studies of degree of leverage hence future studies should include the rate of inflation. In view of that, Gatsi, Gadzo, & Oduro (2016) when conducting a research on the influence on degree of leverage on the financial performance of Ghanaian banks, used the rate of inflation as a controlling variable and found a positive relationship between the rate of inflation and the financial performance of banks in Ghana.

4.3.2 Gross Domestic Product (GDP)

Kosmidou (2008) found that (GDP) growth and major economic factors such as inflation, exchange rate, fuel prices etc has insignificant impact on profitability while GDP and stock market capitalization to assets are significant and have negative relation with the ROA. On the other hand, Mahmud (2003), posit that the relationship between market capitalisation and GDP growth is not linear. This means that, the relationship between degree of leverage and GDP is negative such that the growth of GDP does not influence the degree of leverage positively. Asimakopoulos, Samitas and Papadogonas (2009), find that inflation increases the level of debt, indicating that the effect of the before – tax yield spread between corporate bonds and equities. Because of this, the current study establishes the link between the inflation and its effect on the financial performance on insurance companies in Ghana.

4.3.3 Exchange Rate

Foreign exchange rate an important control variable because it forms part of the overall economic activities and for the past years, the experience in Ghana testifies, exchange rate influences the cost of items in the country. For that matter as the research is focused on the performance of insurance companies who in the end insures against any risk incurred by other companies, they will be affected significantly with the rate of exchange rate. Below are some empirical evidences on the association of foreign exchange rates and performance.

Dong (2011), in a study on foreign exchange rate and degree of leverage decision, recommended that the exchange rate be included in the degree of leverage determinants test, especially when companies in a small economy are studied for which Ghana can is included. In the research it was discovered that, implicit debt are influenced by exchange rate. Some of these risks can be insured through which the financial performance and degree of leverage of the insurance companies can be affected hence the need for the current study. Singapurwoko and El-Wahid (2011) in their research which adopted operational decision factor such as macroeconomics factor, firm size factor, and industry factors to help understand the effect of debt to profitability. The operational decision factor was proxy by total assets turnover to explain how well the companies are able to utilize their assets to generate profit. Firm size factor was proxy by assets to measure the companies' power to generate profit. While macro-economic factor is proxy by bank interest rate because it can represent the inflation effect and the impact to the bank's interest rate.

The uniqueness of their research was to add industry factors to compensate the other factors in determining the companies' profitability. The result indicates that in uncategorized data, debt, firm size, and operational decision effect positively significant, and macroeconomics effect insignificantly towards profitability. In addition, industry factor is found to affect companies' profitability. It must be noted that the results were obtained by considering 48 out of the 228 companies listed on the Indonesian stock exchange and the study also covered a period seven years thus from 2003 to 2009. In a related study on Ghana, Gadzo, Akoto and Gatsi (2013) found that, foreign exchange rate negatively influence the performance of listed banks in Ghana. This conclusion was reach after embarking on a cross sectional data covering 2002 to 2017.

CHAPTER FIVE

EMPIRICAL REVIEW OF FINANCIAL PERFORMANCE AND LEVERAGE OF FIRMS

Learning Objectives

After studying this chapter, you should be able to:

- *identify the empirical relationship between financial performance and degree of leverage*
- *Prepare an analytical framework between financial performance and degree of leverage.*

5.0 Introduction

This empirical review chapter cover issues relating to the relationship that other studies have establish between the financial performance of a firm and the degree of leverage of those firms. A number of empirical studies have identified firm level characteristic and macroeconomic variables that affect degree of leverage and financial performance of firms.

5.1 Relationship between financial performance and the degree of leverage of firms

In examining the association between degree of leverage and firm financial performance, numerous studies have been conducted by researchers that indicate a negative relationship between the two variables by inculcating a controlling variable. These include; the study by Fu (1997), which was on the relationship between degree of leverage and profitability using a cross sectional study on the Malaysian firms. The study was aimed at solving the dearth of research on effect that the degree of leverage has on the profitability of the firms in Malaysia.

In view of that the researcher, took a total of 267 firms listed on the Kuala Lumpur Stock Exchange for a period of ten years from 1985 to 1994. Two major sets of variables were used in the study to indicate degree of leverage. These are Debt to Equity Ratio that was decomposed into Debt Ratio, Financial Leverage Ratio, Funded Capital Ratio, Funded Debt Ratio, Current Debt Ratio, Funded Assets Ratio; and, profitability which was measured by Return On Equity, Earnings Per Share, Return On Investment, Profit Before Tax, Net Income. Using the time-series cross-sectional methodology the data was analysed and in order to generate empirical evidence, the Pearson Product-Moment Correlation, mean and bar chart analysis were employed.

Fu (1997) results implied that profitability is significantly related to degree of leverage. Specifically, profitability was inversely or negatively related to the amount of liability in a company's degree of leverage. Hence, the gearing of the company turns to increase whenever the firms' profitability level reduces. His study also found evidence of the existence of an optimal degree of leverage among listed companies and that firms of different sectors were found to adjust their degree of leverage regularly in order to achieve an optimal combination of debt and equity. Confirming the study by Fu (1997), Lara and Mesquita (2002), who researched into the degree of leverage and profitability in the case of the Brazilian economy, asserts that the determination of degree of leverage for a company is a challenging one that involves several factors, such as risk and profitability. Further in the study Lara and Mesquita (2002) emphasised that the degree of leverage decision becomes even more difficult, in an economy with volatile macroeconomic environment.

Therefore, the choice among the ideal proportion of debt and equity can affect the financial performance of the company, as much as the return rates. In the study, data were collected from 70 companies for a period of seven years. Having indicated the influence of the macro economic factors, the study factored inflation, exchange rate and other economic variable as a controlling variable and therefore used ordinary least Squares (OLS) method in the estimation of a function relating the return on the equity (ROE) with the indexes of long and short-run debts, and also with the total of owner's equity. The results indicated that the return rates present a positive correlation with short-term debt and equity, and an inverse correlation with long-term debt.

The study conducted by Lara and Mesquita (2002), recognised the influence of macroeconomic variable in the choice of degree of leverage as well as the profitability of the firm. This recognition gives credibility to their work because they expanded the discussion to the entire environment unlike what other writers. But the data point in the work as well as the data analysis thus the ordinary least square (OLS) used may not entirely reveal the true situation on the ground.

Kosmidou (2008), in their study, using a panel threshold regression analysis on the degree of leverage and firm value in China which is different from Fu (1997), cross sectional methodology approach found that an increase in gearing does not improve firm value in the same proportion. This conclusion was ascertained by applying an advanced panel threshold regression model to test the panel threshold effect of debt ratio on firm value among 650 A-shares of Chinese listed firms from 2001 to 2006. The results confirm that a triple-threshold effect does exist and showed an inverted-U correlation between leverage and firm value. Attention must be drawn to the fact that, their study did not consider the financial institutions, banking, finance, and insurance firms since they asserted that the balance sheet of those firms has a striking different structure from those of non-financial firms. Though their work did not consider the insurance sector, their study is a significant literature to review because of the panel threshold methodology that was employed by them as the current study also has adapted the panel data methodology.

Moreover, Graf (2010) revealed that, the relationship between the degree of leverage and risk-adjusted profitability of European and US banks is positive. Risk adjusted performance was measured by accounting figures and also by market prices. By using a dynamic panel regression and controlling for several bank characteristics such as loan portfolio quality, liquidity endowment and size. The study found that the bank performance is inversely 'u'-shaped related to the leverage ratio. The leverage ratio for the purpose of the study was defined as total assets over book equity. For the purpose of the study Graf's (2010) analysis was based on banks' balance sheets and income statements between 1994 and 2008 of European and the US banks. A total of 920 data were collected from a sample of about 175 US banks and about 820 observations for 205 European banks. This shows how reliable the study is with reference to the American and the European economies but would have been more generalised if it hand included a sample of financial institutions in both the Asian and the African continent.

In the analysis, the study was analysed with the use of a two-way dynamic panel regression model to relate bank performance to the degree of leverage and the control variables. This meant that the dummy variable for each bank and a dummy variable for each year were appropriately appreciated. That notwithstanding the study also revealed that, but assumption was that the impact of the leverage ratio and the other independent variables on the bank performance is the same across banks and over time. Furthermore, Dreyer (2010) conducted a research that set out to determine whether there is a relationship between the observed leverage levels of South African companies, their profitability, earnings volatility and the probability of financial distress. The study considered the impact of the 2007 and 2008 global financial crisis in the leverage and the earrings volatility and found a negative correlation between the variables which suggests that firms that earn most of their revenue through either imports or exports are subjected to the vicissitude of the South African currency as well as the commodity price cycles. The findings of the study supported both the degree of leverage theory and the pecking order theory.

The results were obtained after taking a population of companies listed on the Johannesburg stock exchange over a period of ten years showing how significant the companies understudy will impact on the findings made. The cross-sectional, longitudinal and panel data methodology was used to analyse the data that was dominated by a secondary data without the consideration of a primary data. Narrowing the issue down to the insurance industry, Ishfaq et al (2010), researched into the determinates of degree of leverage taking the life insurance sector of Pakistan as a case aimed at investigating the impact of firm level characteristics on degree of leverage of life insurance companies of Pakistan so that future studies can understand the factors that influence degree of leverage of the insurance companies.

For the purpose of the study, leverage was taken as dependent variable while profitability, size, growth, age, risk, tangibility of assets and liquidity are selected as independent variables. The result after using the OLS regression model to analyse the data indicated that size, profitability, risk, liquidity and age are important determinants of degree of leverage of life insurance companies and In addition, life insurance companies degree of leverage follow the Pecking order pattern such that profitability, liquidity and age as well as leverage has a negative relationship with degree of leverage while positive relationship between leverage and size shows consistency with the Trade-off theory.

Ishfaq, et al (2010), indicated that one reason that necessitates the usage of less debt ratio is that when firm survives in business for a long time then it accumulates more funds for the day-to-day operations of the business and subsequently keeps away the firm to go for debt financing (Nivorozhkin, 2005). In addition, positive relationship between leverage and age is not likely to apply in transition economies because experience or maturity of the firms before economic reforms is likely to be limited (Al-Bashs & Sentic, 2008).

Their study is consistent with work of Abor (2008) on the issue of determinates of the degree of leverage of firms in Ghana. Therefore, the reason why the researcher has indicated the usage of these variables in the hypothesis formulated for the work. What was not considered by the writers was the factor that would probably affect the performance of the insurance companies

But Ahmad *et al.* (2011) resolved the issue of the determinants of performance of insurance companies by conducting a research on the topic again, discussing it from the perspective of the life insurance sector of Pakistan. The study examined the impact of firm level characteristics such as size, leverage, tangibility, risk, growth, liquidity and age on performance of listed life insurance companies of Pakistan over seven years from 2001 to 2007. The results after conducting an OLS regression analysis indicated that the size, risk and leverage are important determinants of performance of life insurance companies of Pakistan while ROA has statistically insignificant relationship with growth, profitability, age and liquidity. It must be noted that their findings was consistent with the study conducted by the Sufian and Muzafar (2010) and Heng and Ong (2011) to investigate the determinants of profitability by selecting the non-commercial banks financial institutions.

Building on the foundation laid by Ishfaq, *et al.* (2010), Ahmad *et al.* (2011), Petrov and Najjar (2011), conducted a study on the degree of leverage of insurance companies in Bahrain and found a strong relationship between debt ratio variables and profitability of insurance firms. The findings of Petrov and Najjar (2011) was based on 150 insurance companies in Bahrain, most of them are privately held and their financial information is considered confidential and impossible to obtain and for most of them, the integrity of their accounting data cannot be verified due to lack of proper independent auditing. Therefore, the researchers limited the study to all publicly-traded insurance companies listed on the Bahrain Stock Exchange, for a period of 2005-2009 because they publish reliable audited statements. The time period of four years is considered to be short but, that notwithstanding, their model was based on a standard multiple linear regression analysis using the debt ratios as the dependent variables and tangibility of asset, profitability, firm size, revenue growth and liquidity as the independent variable. Though their work is referred as the ground breaking for studies into the degree of leverage of insurance companies, their profitability was measured with only return on asset without any giving any justification for that action.

In relation to the Ghanaian context, studies by Amidu (2007), Abor's (2008) and Abor and Beikpe (2009) have established an inverse relationship between short-term debt and firm profitability. Abor (2008) found an inverse relationship between company profitability and long-term debt. Graham and Leary (2010) concluded that there is an inverse relationship between total debt and profitability. He further indicated that large and profitable companies present low debt levels. Furthermore Akoto and Gatsi (2010), entered into the financial industry of Ghana by conducting a study of the degree of leverage and profitability in Ghanaian banks using panel data methodology. The study covered banks listed on the Ghana stock exchange (GES) and covered a period ten years and was observed that 87 percent of the total capital of banks in Ghana is made up of debt. 65 percent of the debt component constitutes short-term debts while the remaining is made up of long-term debts.

Their findings however, confirmed that banks are highly levered institutions and also highlights the significance of short term debts over long-term debts in bank financing in Ghana. Their finding was in consonance with previous studies in Ghana by Amidu (2007) in stressing the importance of short term debt in firm financing in Ghana. Akoto and Gatsi (2010) also, revealed a significant negative relationship between bank size and profitability and made the suggestion that larger banks tend to exhibit lower margins and is consistent with models that emphasize the negative role of size from scale inefficiencies. Akoto and Gatsi (2010) also revealed a significantly negative association between short-term debts and net interest margin. This means that as deposits increase in the banking sector, net interest margin falls. In their study, long-term debts were negative but insignificant in determining net interest margin in the banking sector. Regarding total debts, it was significant and negatively related to net interest margin. Finally their study revealed that bank size was significantly and negatively related to both returns on equity and net interest margin in the banking sector. However there was a positive and statistically significant relationship between sales growth and both returns on equity and net interest margin in the banking sector.

Akoto and Gatsi (2010) concluded that short-term debts, long term-debts, and total debt are insignificant in determining returns on equity (ROE) in the banking sector of Ghana. The researchers attributed this to the increased cost of undertaking banking business in Ghana coupled with underutilization of deposits due to high lending rates.

Though their study covered a significant number of years, if they had considered the insurance sector, it would have provided a complete assertion of the degree of leverage situation of the financial sector in Ghana and therefore would have helped helps improve the decision making by authorities in that regard; In order to reveal the nature of the degree of leverage of the insurance sector, the current study is to be conducted on the situation. But not all the empirical studies indicate the existence of a negative relationship between degree of leverage and profitability rather some equally reveal a positive relationship such that degree of leverage move along with the profitability of the companies.

Even though the above empirical evidence indicates a negative association between leverage and profitability, other researchers are of a different view. These researchers in their studies found a positive association between profitability and leverage. For example Champion (1999) and Barclay and Clifford (2005) argue that companies can use more debt to enhance their financial performance because of debts capability to cause managers to improve productivity to avoid bankruptcy. Afterwards, Mazur (2007) in a regression analysis of four profitability metrics against debt ratio observed a significantly positive relationship between debt and profitability. To add to what has already been discussed, publications by researchers in the area of finance have also supported the notion that there exists a significantly positive relation between profitability and firm leverage (Cheng, Chein & Liu, 2010). Pratheepkanth (2011), also revealed the existence of a positive association between debt and return on equity of firms provided that, the earnings power of the firm's assets outweighs the average interest cost of the debt.

To further improve on the studies conducted earlier on, Singapurwoko and El-Wahid (2011) studied on the impact of financial leverage to profitability study of non-financial companies listed in Indonesia Stock Exchange and revealed that, Debt is used by many companies to leverage their capital and profit. However, debt is not the only factors that affect degree of leverage and profit. From a current perspective, Abu-Rub (2012) in the study that investigated the impact of degree of leverage on firm performance. The study use five performance measures which are return on equity, return on assets, earning per share, market value of equity to the book value of equity and Tobin's Q as dependent variable and four degree of leverage measures which are short – term debt, long-term debt and total debt to total assets, and total debt to total equity as independent variable.

The analysis of the investigation was performed using panel data procedure for a sample of 28 listed companies the Palestinian Stock Exchange over the period of 2006-2010.

The results revealed that firm's degree of leverage has a positive impact on the firm's performance measures, in both the accounting and market's measures, and statistically significant with total debt to total asset except market value of equity and book value of equity was significant with total debt to total asset and with short term debt to total asset.

Finally, the study findings suggested equations to determine the impact of the various debts on the firm performance which was missed from the studies conducted by earlier researchers in the field. In the Ghanaian context, a study designed to examine the effect of degree of leverage on profitability of listed firms in Ghana, Abor (2005) observed a significantly positive relationship between the ratio of short-term debt to total assets and profitability, but a negative association between the ratio of long term debt to total assets and profitability. It should be noted that in conclusion, Abor (2005) reported a significantly positive relationship between total debt and profitability thus supporting the above previous works.

The conclusion drawn from these empirical works suggests that companies with high future returns use more debt relative to equity in funding their operations. Also from the foregoing discussions based on the available empirical literature, it is evident that the results from the investigations into the relationship between degree of leverage and profitability are inconclusive, and requires more empirical work. The researcher therefore believes that, the knowledge of how degree of leverage affects financial performance of the insurance sector of Ghana would enhance efficient and prudent financing decision which would in turn make the insurance competitive.

5.2 Analytical Framework

Based on the literature reviewed, an analytical framework which is demonstrated in Figure 1 has been developed. The independent variable in this study is degree of leverage and the dependent variable is financial performance. The relationship between degree of leverage and financial performance is such that they are inversely related as was noted by scholars like Fama and French (2005), Ahmad, Naveed and Zulfqar (2011) whose studies provided empirical evidence supporting this negative relationship between debt levels and a firm's performance.

Figure 5.1: Analytical framework

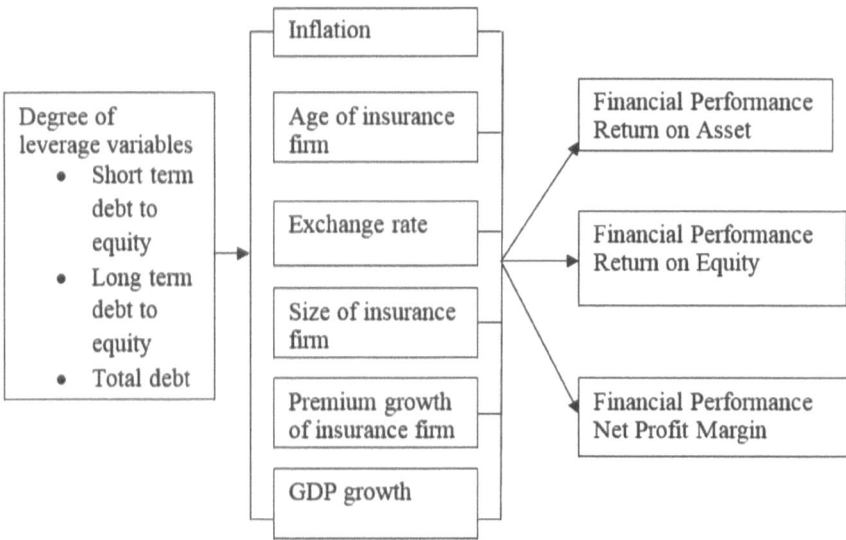

Source: Constructed from Literature 2018

The relationship between the independent and controlling variables is such that there is an inverse relationship between degree of leverage and firm size and a positive relationship between degree of leverage and macro-economic variables as was indicated by Petrov and Najjar (2011), El-Wahid and Singapurwoko (2011) and Gatsi, (2012). In this study, the researcher expects a significantly negative relationship between short-term debt to capital ratio and the three profitability matrices. This relationship is expected so as to meet the dictates of theoretical and durational matching perspectives in the insurance companies in Ghana.

Also, in this study the researcher rather expects a negative relationship between long –term debt and the three profitability matrices. With regard to the controlling variables, size and profitability relationship is expected to be negative. A statistical negative and significant association with the dependent variables will imply the existence of the scale inefficiency hypothesis insurance companies in Ghana.

Again, in the present study, a negative relationship is also expected between the dependent variables and sales growth. The negative relationship between the dependent variables and sales indicates that, non-financial firms in Ghana do not really gain much from their core businesses. Although the literature reviewed above empirically show support for the pecking order theory, other writers are of different opinion such that most of them have found either a positive relationship or a negative relationship to exist among the degree of leverage and financial performance of the companies. It is therefore clear from the empirical literature that earlier studies done to determine the association between total debt and firm's profitability are inconclusive. In this study, the researcher also expects a negative relationship between total debt and firm's profitability as depicted by Figure 5.1.

CHAPTER SIX

RESEARCH METHODS

Learning Objectives

After studying this chapter, you will be able to understand the:

- *research design and population used for the study*
- *sampling procedure and data collection procedures*
- *estimation of the variables used for the study*
- *estimation model and technique*

6.0 Introduction

This section presents the methods that the researcher used in executing the study by discussing the research design, the population, the sample and the sampling procedure. It also discusses the sources of data collection, variables used, the panel regression model and the data analyses plan.

6.1 Research Design

Bui (2009), posits that research can be categorised into exploratory, descriptive and causal. The exploratory research is conducted to obtain a better understanding on issues that the research problem revolve around, while descriptive research tries to describe the features of a phenomenon. Causal research is used to identify the causes and effect relationships between the main variable under study. Based on this explanation, this study can be classified as causal in nature as it sought to explain the cause-and-effect relationships between degree of leverage variables and profitability variables. But because the current data set is in a panel form, the panel model is used. According to Park (2009), panel data models examine group and individual-specific effects, time effects, or both. He further added that, effects are either fixed effect or random effect. A fixed effect model examines if intercepts vary across groups or time periods, whereas a random effect model explores differences in error variances.

Again the study sought to find the difference in the degree of leverage practices and the level of financial performance among insurance companies whose age are below twenty years and those whose age are above the age of twenty during the period of study. To effectively attain this goal the analysis of variance (ANOVA) was used to test this relationship between groups since Bui (2009) indicated that analysis of variance is the best means of testing whether the means of two groups are significantly the same of not.

In addition, Akoto and Gatsi (2010) posit that, panel data involves the pooling of observations on cross-section of units over several time periods. Therefore, since this study involve the pooling of observation on cross-section of units over a period of five years; it lends its self to panel data form. Besides, the model effectively addresses the objectives of the study. From this backdrop, almost all data used in this study were quantitative hence it becomes appropriate to classify the study as a quantitative research.

Cooper and Schindler (2001) explained that, quantitative research methodology relates to numbers and measuring of observed facts. They also argue that quantitative research methodology permits specification of dependents variable and allows for longitudinal measures of subsequent performance of the research subject. The method is compatible with the study because it allows the research problem to be conducted in a very specific and set terms. Besides, the approach plainly and distinctively specifies both the independent and the dependent variables under investigation. It also follows resolutely the original set of research goals, arriving at a more objective conclusion, testing hypothesis, determining the issues of causality and eliminate or minimize subjectivity of judgments.

6.2 Population for the study

A population is any complete group of entities sharing some common set of characteristics (Zikmund 1997). In view of this, the population understudy could be defined as all general insurance companies in Ghana which had their complete sets of financial statement with the National Insurance Commission from the year 2002 to 2017. For this reason the population for the study was 18. The reason why only general insurance companies was used for the study is that, for the period studied the complete financial statement for the life insurance companies were not obtained for 2002 to 2017. The target population for this study is made up of 25 insurance firms as recorded in the national insurance commission report for 2017.

6.3 Sampling and Sampling Procedure

The purposive sampling technique was used to purposely select insurance companies in Ghana from 2002 to 2017 to constitute the sampling frame for the study. According Bui (2009), purposive sampling refers to the process through which a group of representative individuals is selected from a population to meet the purpose of the study. This technique was appropriate because the insurance companies which had their financial statements with the Ghana National Insurance Commission (GNIC) between the period of 2002 and 2011 was eighteen which relative small for a sample to be selected for the study.

6.4 Data collection Procedure

This study involved only secondary data; specifically the financial statement of insurance companies between the periods of 2002 to 2017. The secondary data according to Saunders, Lewis, and Thornhill (2007) are made of three groups which are survey-based data, documentary data, and those compiled from multiple sources. The survey based data describes data, which has been collected through survey strategies, such as the use of questionnaires. Therefore, survey-based secondary data is useful for studies that require data that has already been collected for similar studies. Documentary data comprises memos, news, reports and administrative correspondence that hold information that is critical for the study. On the other hand, Cheng, Chien and Liu (2010), mentioned that, multiple-source secondary data relates to data collected through the combination of survey-based data and documentary data.

Three reasons informed the choice for secondary data for the study. Firstly the data required for the study could not be procured through primary source because the holders of the data were not willing to release the data. Secondly, the financial performance data of most companies can be obtained from their either their published or unpublished financial statements which offered a basis for their analysis. Finally, an authentic overview of the degree of leverage of a given company emanates from the appropriate degree of leverage ratios which can only be computed from the financial statement for a given period. The data set for the study are classified into two categories; financial data which were obtained from the data file of National Insurance Commission and the economic data were accessed from the data file of the Ghana Statistical Service

6.5 Measurement of variables

Quantitative studies seek to give a precise and objective report about a phenomenon; and as such the need to measure the attributes of the phenomenon in quantitative studies (Bui 2009). As described in the study design, this study is quantitative and for that matter, it is important to specify how both the dependent (Return on Asset, Return on Equity and Net Profit margin) and the independent variables (short term debt to total capital ratio, long term debt to total capital ratio, total debt to total capital ratio, age of company, size of company, premium growth, inflation, exchange rage and GDP.

6.5.1 Dependent variables

Three dependent variables, namely, return on asset (ROA), return on equity (ROE) and net profit margin (NPM) were used to assess profitability of the insurance companies in the study. These ratios according to Ross, Westerfield, Jeff and Jordan (2011) are computed as shown in Appendix C.

6.5.1.1 Return on asset

Return on asset (ROA) was estimated as the ratio of net income that is after tax profit per Ghana cedi of asset to total asset. This ratio measures after tax profit per cedi of assets. It is also called return on investment (ROI).

6.5.1.2 Return on equity

The return on equity (ROE) was defined as the product of ROA and equity multiplier. Where ROA is a measure of financial performance linked to the asset size of the insurance companies while the equity multiplier which explains the extent to which the assets of insurance companies are funded with equity relative to debt is a measure of leverage (Saunders and Cornett, 2004). Due to this fact the hypothesis for the study was tested using ROE as the financial performance as it inculcates the return on asset in it value. The use of ROE as a profitability measure was appropriate due to the fact that ROE represents the return that goes to the owners of a business. This assisted the researcher in distinguishing the returns specifically to the owners as against returns to the whole firm.

6.5.1.3 Net profit margin

The third dependent variable is the ratio of net profit margin. It is the profit that is available from each cedi of sales after all expenses have been paid, including cost of goods, selling and administrative expenses, dependable interest and taxes (Westerfield, Jeff & Jordan (2011). Literature on corporate finance indicates that ROE is generally preferred to ROA and NPM as a profitability indicator (Dreyer, 2010). Nonetheless, the researcher considered NPM as other dependent variables in the study since it reflects the profit that emanates from the core business or sales of the firms and thus the researcher will desire to see how the explanatory variables would influence it in the regression model.

6.5.2 The Independent Variables

Five main independent variables were considered for the study. They are; short-term debt to total capital, long-term debt to total capital, total debt to total capital, firm size, premium growth and the age of the firms. The other variables such as inflation, gross domestic product and exchange rate were used as controlling variable as employed by El-Wahid and Singapurwoko (2011) in their research into the impact of financial leverage to profitability study of non-financial companies listed in Indonesia stock exchange.

6.5.2.1 The ratio of short-term debt to total capital

This ratio is defined as the ratio of short-term debt to total capital. It is considered to measure the extent to which the insurance companies under study use short –term debt to finance their operations and how this category of debt associates with the firm's profitability for the chosen period of the study.

Abor (2008) and Amidu (2007) established that firms use a significant amount of short term debt to finance their activities relative to long term debts. According to Abor (2008) there exist a significantly positive association between company profitability and short-term debt to total capital ratio. Amidu (2007) however observed an inverse relationship between short-term debt to capital and firm profitability.

6.5.2.2 The ratio of long-term debt to total capital

This is the ratio of long-term debt to total capital. It measures the extent to which insurance companies use long-term debt to finance their operations and how this category of debts associates with the firm's profitability for the chosen period of the study. Abor (2008) and Amidu (2007) established that firms use a relatively lesser amount of long-term debt to time their activities relative to short-term debt. Abor (2008) indicated that there is an inverse relationship between company profitability and long –term debt to capital ratio. It should however be noted that Amidu (2007) observed a positive association between long-term debt and a firm's profitability.

6.5.2.3 The ratio of total debt to total capital

This is the ratio of total liabilities to total capital. Basically it is the summation of short term debt and long term debt of the firms to their total capital. This ratio measures the extent to which the operations of the firms have been funded with total debt relative to equity and also to see how leverage associates with insurance companies' financial performance in Ghana. Many studies have been conducted to determine the relationships between leverage and profitability showed a positive association. (Graham & Leary, 2010)

6.5.3 Firm Specific Variables

Firm level characteristics refer to those variables that are used to describe the specific feature of the organisation (Abor, 2005). This definition is what was adopted as the operational definition for the study. For the purpose of the study the firm specific variables are measured by Firm size, premium growth and the age of the insurance companies. This decision is based on the empirical results discussed in the literature review. These firm specific variables are explained below.

6.5.3.1 Firm size

Size has been viewed as a determinant of a firm's degree of leverage (Abor, 2008). Larger firms tend to be more diversified and hence have lower variance of earnings, making them able to tolerate high debt ratios (Mazur, 2007). Smaller firms on the other hand may find it relatively more costly to resolve information asymmetric with lenders thus may present lower debt ratios (Saad, 2010). In this study, firm size has been taken as the logarithm of the total asset of the insurance companies. The use of logarithm enables us to obtain the real total asset of the firms due to its capabilities to standardize values thus, bringing them on the same platform for a more efficient analysis to be done.

6.5.3.2 Premium growth

The relationship between premium growth and degree of leverage can also be explained by pecking order hypothesis. Growing firms place a greater demand on the internally generated funds of the firm (Abor, 2005). Asimakopoulos, Samitas and Papadogonas (2009) argued that firms with high growth will capture relatively higher debt ratios. Dreyer (2010) further stated that, there is also a relationship between the degree of previous growth and future growth. Abu-Rub (2012) however, argues that firms with growth opportunities will have smaller proportions of the debt in their degree of leverage. This is due to the fact that, conflict between debt and equity holders are especially serious for assets that give the firm that option to undertake such growth opportunities in the future.

6.5.3.3 Age of firm

The age of the firm basically estimate how old the insurance company has been in existence since its establishment. This is to clearly explain the effect of the degree of leverage of old aged and young insurance companies on their financial performance. In the study, earning before tax profit was used instead of after tax profit or net income, for the computation of the profitability ratios so that the result of the estimation is prevented from being distorted by the influence of tax payment.

Usually profit making firms pay taxes proportional to the profit made for the period. This presupposes that the higher the profit the higher the tax charge, and the lower the profit the lower the tax charged. As a result the researcher believes that using after tax profit as a numerator in computing the profitability ratios for the insurance firms in Ghana for the chosen period of study may therefore not reflect the true and fair financial performance of the insurance companies.

6.5.4 Macroeconomic indicators

The macro economic variables for the purpose of the study are inflation, gross domestic product and the exchange rate. The inflation is used for the study because it represents price stability which affects the premium charges of the insurance companies. Again, gross domestic product is chosen because it represents the amounts of goods and services that an economy produce in a given economy over a given period of time. Finally exchange rate that was used was the rate of exchange between the Ghana cedi and the United State dollars. The United State dollars was used because according to the

GSS report (2017), about 80 percent of the foreign transactions in Ghana is made through the United State dollars.

6.6 Panel regression model

The panel regression model used by Abor (2008), Akoto and Gatsi (2010) and Ahmad, Naveed and Zulfquar (2011) was adopted for this study. Abor (2008) indicated that panel data provides results that are simply not detectable in pure cross-sections or pure time-series studies. Abor (2008) further argued that the panel data is more useful than either cross-section or time series data as used by Fu (2007) alone due to the following reasons;

Firstly, panel data model provides more edifying data, more variability, less collinearly among variables, more degrees of freedom and more effectiveness. Also, the model provides controls for individual's heterogeneity due to hidden factors. The panel data model again provides better ability to study dynamics of adjustments. Furthermore, the model generates better ability to identify effects that are simply not detectable in pure cross –section or pure time-series data and finally panel data model enable the researcher to construct and test more complicated behavioural models then cross-section on or time-section data.

6.7 Model specification for firm specific variable's

The theoretical and empirical literature on degree of leverage in finance has identified a vector of variables that influence firm financial performance including debt, disintegrated into short-term debt, long term debt, and total debt. The relationship between debt and insurance companies financial performance in Ghana is thus estimated in the following regression models:

$$\gamma_{i,t} = \beta_0 + \beta_1 STD_{I,T} + \beta_2 SZ_{I,T} + \beta_3 PG_{IT} + \beta_4 AG_{I,t} + e \quad \text{...........................(1)}$$

$$\gamma_{i,t} = \beta_0 + \beta_1 LTD_{I,T} + \beta_2 SZ_{I,T} + \beta_3 PG_{IT} + \beta_4 AG_{I,t} + e \quad \text{...........................(2)}$$

$$\gamma_{i,t} = \beta_0 + \beta_1 TD_{I,T} + \beta_2 SZ_{I,T} + \beta_3 PG_{IT} + \beta_4 AG_{I,t} + e_{it} \quad \text{...........................(3)}$$

Where:

$\gamma_{i,t}$ Represents Return on Assets, Return on Equity and Net Profit Margin for firm i in time t ; while STD, LTD,TD, SZ, PG and AG represents Short Term Debts to capital ratio ;Long Term Debts to capital ratio ; Total Debt to capital ratio; Firm Size; Premium Growth; age of the insurance companies and *e* is the error term

6.8 Model specification for macroeconomic variable's

The theoretical and empirical literature on degree of leverage in finance has identified a vector of variables that influence firm financial performance including macroeconomic variables, disintegrated into gross domestic product, inflation and exchange rate. The relationship between macroeconomic variables and financial performance of the insurance companies in Ghana is thus estimated in the following regression models:

$$\gamma = \beta_0 + \beta_2 IF_{I,T} + \beta_3 GDP_{I,T} + \beta_4 EX_{I,t} + e \quad \ldots\ldots(4)$$

Where:

γ Represents Return on Assets, Return on Equity and Net Profit Margin

IF represent inflation; GDP represent gross domestic product; EX represent exchange rate and *e* is the error term

6.9 Estimation method

Park (2009) opined that estimation of panel data models using pooled ordinary least squares yields inconsistent estimators and heteroskedasticity errors. The researcher further stated that if the parameters to be estimated vary across firms the pooled regression is not appropriate because of the heterogeneity in the parameter as an estimate is not well dealt with. From a theoretically perspective, Baltagi (2005), explained that overlooking such stricture heterogeneity among cross –sectional and time series could lead to inconsistency estimates of interesting parameters. Baltagi (2005) noted that correct this problem, it is therefore appropriate to use panel data model. According to the researcher, panel estimation methods including the fixed effect and random effect methods are commonly used in estimating heteroskedastic consistent estimators. Park (2009), further stated the basic differences between the above mentioned estimation technique was based on the assumption about the relationship between the error term and the covariates. The choice of the estimation process is informed by the deficiencies with pooled ordinary least squares.

Using panel data to estimate models requires the determination of whether there is a correlation between the unobservable heterogeneity in each firm and the explanatory variables of the model. If the final outcome results a correlation which is fixed effect, consistent estimation would be obtained by means of the group estimation. Otherwise, random effects are more appropriate estimator that can be achieved by estimating the equation by cross section generalized least squares (Park, 2009). The usual econometrics strategy to determine whether the effects are fixed or random is to use the Hausman (1978) test under the null hypothesis. If the null hypothesis is rejected, the effects are measured to be fixed, and the model is then estimated by OLS. If the null hypothesis is accepted, we would have random effects, and the model is then estimated by GLS. In this way we achieve a more efficient estimator of β and the estimated model can be said to be robust, all else equal. But because the some of the independent variables might have multicollinearity the ordinary ridge regression is used in the study. Park (2009) indicated that, ordinary ridge regression (ORR) is used to correct the problem of multicollinearity though it has the problem of shrinking the estimates toward zero.

6.10 Data preparation and analysis plan

The quantitative data from the financial statements of the insurance companies from 2002 to 2017 was used for the study. Two main ratios, the profitability ratio and the leverage ratios were computed using the raw data from the financial statements in accordance with the formulae provided under "measurement of variables". The profitability ratios computed were return on assets (ROA), return on equity (ROE) and net profit margin (NPM). The leverage ratios computed were short –term debt to total capital, long –term debt to total capital, and total debt to total capital. Other variables that were computed were the firm size, premium growth and ages of the firms.Since the study is quantitative in nature, four main sections were considered for discussion under the analysis column. First, the descriptive statistics of the variables, then the multi collinearity matrix and finally the results of the panel regression estimate of profitability and debt nexus conclude the discussion.

6.11 Summary

This section of the study described how the research was undertaken, it stated with the research design of which the casual design was settled for the study. The population and its respective sampling size was also describe after which how the variables were measured also followed suit. The section ended with the measurement and estimation models used for the study.

CHAPTER SEVEN

NATURE OF DEGREE OF LEVERAGE AMONG INSURANCE COMPANIES IN GHANA

Learning Objectives

By the of the chapter, the reader will be able to;

- *provide a description of the variables*
- *comprehend the nature of the degree of leverage among insurance companies in Ghana*

7.1 Introduction

This chapter presents the discussion on the nature of the degree of leverage among insurance companies in Ghana. The findings are based on the panel data methodology discussed in chapter six. The chapter is divided into three main sections. The first section deals with the descriptive statistics of the dependent, independent as well as the controlling variables used in the study as shown in Table 7.1 The second section is focused on the nature of degree of leverage among insurance companies in Ghana as shown in Tables 7.2, 7.3 and 7.4. This is followed by Table 7.5 which discusses the group statistics of degree of leverage of the insurance companies while Tables 7.6 and 7.7 explains the trend in the financial performance indicator and ANOVA of the degree of leverage indicators respectively for the two groups that are insurance companies which are aged below 20 and those insurance companies which are aged above 20 during the period of 2002 to 2017.

7.2 Descriptive statistics

Table 7.1 provides a summary of the descriptive statistics of the dependent and independent variables which were measured in percentages. It shows the average indicators of the variables computed from the financial statements of insurance companies in Ghana from 2002 to 2017 as well as the some macro-economic variables of the economy of Ghana during the 16 year period. The list of the insurance companies is shown in Appendix A. As indicated in the methodology, twelve (12) variables, consisting of three dependent and nine explanatory variables were considered for the study.

Table 7.1: Descriptive Statistics

	N	Min	Max	Mean	Std. Deviation	Skewness
ROA	288	-64.00	12	9.13	14.89	3.00
ROE	288	-10.00	14	14.78	25.46	0.80
NPM	288	-70.80	17	11.80	15.65	4.64
STD	288	5.46	87.21	50.86	27.91	5.84
LTD	288	0.00	54.90	9.76	11.51	1.02
TD	288	11.95	35.00	60.53	27.20	6.71
Firm Size	288	4.77	10.88	6.97	0.69	0.53
Sales Growth	288	-41.03	65.48	19.26	19.16	0.87
Inflation rate	288	8.58	23.60	14.03	4.37	0.72

Degree of Leverage: Empirical analysis from the insurance sector

GDP	288	4.50	13.60	6.74	2.53	1.89
Exchange rate	288	0.84	1.93	1.12	0.330	1.34
Age	288	3.00	87.00	24.06	17.44	2.06

Source: Financial Statements of Insurance Companies

From the descriptive statistic table, it is observed that the average ROA for the insurance companies is 9.13 percent which is above the industry average of 2 percent and 4 percent for 2016 and 2017respectively, as indicated in the National Insurance Commission report (2017) for general insurance companies. This is an indicative of competition in the insurance industry; hence companies in the industry should adopt forward-looking strategies to remain profitable amidst the level of competition in that industry.

ROE which average 14.78 percent over the study period was also above the industry average of 4 percent and 5 percent for 2016 and 2017 as indicted in the National Insurance Commission report for 2017. This implies that on the average shareholders of the insurance companies received a return of 14.78 percent on their investment. The relatively high NPM of about 11.80 percent may be attributed to the premium collected throughout the period as well as the corresponding reduction in claims paid by the insurance companies as reported by the National Insurance Commission Report of 2017.

The degree of leverage variables reveal consistent results with other literatures that have been conducted on the insurance companies over the world such as (Ishfaq et al, 2010; Najjar and Petrov, 2011; Dhanasekaran et al. 2012). During the period of 2002 to 2017, the short-term debt to total capital ratio averaged 50.86 percent. However, the long-term debt to total capital ratio stood at 9.76 percent. Total debt averaged 60.53 percent.

This is an indication that approximately 61 percent of total assets in the insurance sector of Ghana are financed by debt, confirming the fact that insurance companies debt level are slightly above average levered institutions (Najjar & Petrov, 2011; Dhanasekaran, Kumar,

Sandhya & Saravanan, 2012). A significant observation is that, over 51 percent of these are short-term debts, attesting to the fact that Ghanaian insurance companies largely depend on short-term debt for financing their business. This trend is also famous as a result of the under-developed nature of the Ghanaian long-term debt market, which makes it difficult for most Ghanaian insurance companies to access long-term debt.

From Table 7.1; there is a positive relationship between the premium collected by insurance companies and the respective claim payments. This implies that with increase claim payment, insurance companies may have to diversify their business portfolio to increase non premium income such as investment in new business rather than the insurance products offering. The average firm size and premium growth of 6.97 percent and 19.26 percent seems to be in consonance with the results of earlier studies conducted in the insurance sector of Pakistan (Ahmad, Naveed & Zulfquar, 2011).

7.3 Nature of degree of leverage

To effectively describe the nature of the degree of leverage being practiced by insurance companies in Ghana, the insurance companies were categorised into two based on their ages. This is because Abor (2008) indicated the effect of ages of firms on the degree of leverage of insurance companies.

Table 7.2: Short term debt to total capital average of the studied entities form 2002 – 2017

Years	Insurance Company Classification by Age		
	Below 20 years	Above 20 years	Total
2002	60.09	50.70	55.40
2003	63.32	54.36	58.58
2004	63.83	49.97	59.90
2005	83.18	52.74	67.96
2006	63.43	53.26	58.35
2007	50.21	41.76	45.99
2008	47.89	36.33	42.11
2009	31.36	39.23	35.29
2010	33.67	48.19	40.93
2011	54.24	36.08	45.16
2012	37.07	36.62	36.68
2013	33.78	34.87	34.08
2014	30.50	33.12	31.48
2015	27.22	31.36	28.88
2016	23.94	29.61	26.29
2017	20.65	27.86	23.69

Source: Financial Statements of Insurance Companies

One of the groups represented, companies with age above 20 years while the other group represented companies with age below 20 years. The nature of degree of leverage is descried for all the degree of leverage measures used in the study.

From Table 7.2, short term debts take a higher fraction of the degree of leverage of insurance companies in Ghana. According to the classification of the insurance companies, the companies whose ages are above 20 years had the minimal proportion of short term debt in their degree of leverage than those whose ages are above 20 years. The inclination of debts which are of short term nature in the degree of leverage of the classifications persist in increase from 2002 to 2005 where the insurance companies with age below 20 attained an all-time high of 83.18 percent of short term debt the other group had its largest proportion of 53.67 percent in 2006.

The trend of the preference for short term debt decline thereafter, this is because since 2006 as depicted in Table 7.2, the total average short term debt were below 50 percent of the degree of leverage of the insurance companies. Notwithstanding this evidence, the insurance companies which have been in operational existence for more than two decades, had about 50 percent of short term debt in their degree of leverage than those less than two decades. The rationale for this can be credited to the regulation by the Ghana National insurance commission which decreed a change of the composite insurance to the division of general insurance and life insurance. The implication of this is that, due to the division the insurance companies might not have the collateral for the contraction of short term debt.

Table 7.3 describes the average proportion of long term debt in the degree of leverage of insurance companies in Ghana. Unlike the nature of the short term debt, where insurance companies whose age are below 20 years have the highest proportion of short term debt in their degree of leverage than those whose age are above 20 years, the nature of long term debt in the degree of leverage of the insurance companies shows an inverse situation.

Table 7.3: Long term debt to total capital ratio average of the studied entities form 2002 – 2017

	Insurance Company Classification by Age		
Year	Below 20 years	Above 20 years	Total
2002	6.87	9.50	8.18
2003	6.49	8.41	7.51
2004	6.68	9.42	8.05
2005	10.30	10.17	10.24
2006	14.69	10.00	12.35
2007	13.64	12.89	13.27
2008	5.68	11.87	8.78
2009	9.60	11.57	10.59
2010	6.11	8.65	7.38
2011	7.36	13.36	10.36
2012	8.79	12.42	10.60
2013	8.80	12.76	10.77
2014	8.81	13.09	10.94
2015	8.82	13.43	11.11
2016	8.82	13.76	11.28
2017	8.83	14.09	11.45

Source: Financial Statements of Insurance Companies

From Table 7.3, none of the years recorded more that 20 percent proportion of long term debt in the degree of leverage of the insurance companies. This implies that, the practice of high long term debt in the insurance companies in Ghana is not common and that insurance companies in Ghana prefer less than 20 percent of their debt structure to be long term in nature so that they are not exposed to the bankruptcy cost and the financial distress attached to the use of long term debt.

Again, form Table 7.3, while the proportion of long term debt capital continues to increase for the insurance companies whose age are below twenty thus from 6.87 percent in 2002 to 14.69 percent in

Degree of Leverage: Empirical analysis from the insurance sector

2006, that of insurance companies whose age are above twenty had their long term debt fluctuating during the period understudy and because the proportion of long term debt of this group is larger than the insurance companies whose age are below twenty, it translated into the total average of the proportion of long term debt in the degree of leverage of the insurance companies with statistics of 8.18 percent in 2002; 8.05 percent in 2004; 12.35 percent in 2008 and 10.36 percent in 2011Table 7.4 indicates the total debt structure of insurance companies sampled for the current study.

Table 7.4: Total term debt to total capital ratio average of the studied entities form 2002 – 2017

Years	Insurance Company Classification by Age		
	Below 20years	Above 20 years	Total
2002	66.96	60.21	63.58
2003	69.81	62.77	66.08
2004	70.51	59.38	64.95
2005	83.63	62.33	84.16
2006	75.16	64.23	72.53
2007	63.93	55.32	61.73
2008	56.53	43.92	51.38
2009	43.73	42.64	42.26
2010	36.79	53.32	44.24
2011	56.57	57.18	56.59
2012	43.99	48.09	46.14
2013	40.65	46.63	43.48
2014	37.31	45.16	40.82
2015	33.97	43.70	38.17
2016	30.63	42.24	35.51
2017	27.29	40.78	32.85

Source: Financial Statements of Insurance Companies

Degree of Leverage: Empirical analysis from the insurance sector

From the table, the proportion of debt in the degree of leverage of insurance companies in Ghana was higher than equity capital until the periods of 2009 and 2010 where the proportion of total debt in the degree of leverage recorded, 42.26 percent and 44.24 percent respectively. The import of this is that, the components of equity in the degree of leverage during those periods were more than that of debt capital. This is in consonance with the implication of the pecking order theory as described by Barlay and Clifford (2005), that companies which have quit a substantial free cash will have a low debt capital because the free cash will be used to settle the debts and still have some reserves for the management of the for the operational activities of the company.

The nature of the degree of leverage among the companies with age below 20 and those with age above 20 are the same with both groups having a higher proportion of debt capital than equity capital. But a stunning examination of the total debt to total capital statistics in Table 7.4 shows that the level of total debt in the capital began to decline in 2007 thus from 61.73 to 56.59 in 2011. The reason could be attributed to the reregulation of the National Insurance Act in 2007 which required insurance companies to separate general insurance business from the life insurance business because of the seemingly different nature of their activities.

This is because from Table 7.4 the age of the insurance companies can be said to have a positive impact on the nature of the degree of leverage such that, as they grow, they retain some of their earnings and use them in financing their activities. The import of this is that as the insurance companies which are currently below the age of 20 attain the age of twenty and above they are likely to reduce debt capital in their degree of leverage implying that, this nature is consistent with the static trade off theory whish asserts that firms with a greater risk of experiencing financial distress will borrow less than firms with a lower risk of financial distress.

Table 7.5 indicates the group statistics of the insurance companies as they are grouped into two with one group showing the nature of the degree of leverage of insurance companies who are aged below 20 and the other group showing those companies which are aged above 20 to ascertain the degree of leverage practice among the insurance companies understudy. From Table 7.5, insurance companies with age below 20 years have more debt component in their degree of leverage than those companies aging above 20 with a coefficient of 64.06 percent and 56.99 percent respectively for the two groups.

ANOVA between insurance companies classified by age
Table 7.5: Group statistics for ANOVA

	Age Category	Mean	Std. Deviation	Std. Error Mean
Total Debt to Total Capital Ratio	Below 20years	64.06	35.75	3.79
	Above 20 years	56.99	14.11	1.49

Source: Financial Statements of Insurance Companies

This implies that within the first two decade of the establishment of insurance companies in Ghana, insurance companies' contract debt capital to withstand the competition as well as their survival but with time they learn from the learning curve experience and accumulate earnings for their day to day operations hence. This seems to be in line with the pecking order theory discussed by Watson and Head (2010) and Ross, Westerfield, Jeff and Jordan (2011).

The reason for this been that as insurance companies grow in Ghana, they become capable of generating equity finance through the private placement market. By reason of their size and business track record, they may also have an equal access to the debt market other listed firms. Table 7.6, explains the trend in the financial performance indicators between the insurance companies aged below 20 and those above 20 to establish the trend in the return on equity of the insurance companies linking it to the change in the regulation of the insurance industries in 2007. The Insurance Act 2006, ACT 724 prohibits composite insurance companies, all composite insurance companies therefore had to separate their life and nonlife operations into different companies by December 2007

Table 7.6: Trend of Return on Equity

Year	Insurance companies classification by age	
	Below 20years	Above 20 years
2002	10.33	11.33
2003	7.75	15.78
2004	16.00	10.44
2005	35.81	10.70
2006	8.38	18.65
2007	23.46	20.56
2008	21.47	19.67
2009	9.09	10.67
2010	-2.38	9.67
2011	4.44	8.67
2012	7.22	12.39
2013	6.09	12.17
2014	4.96	11.94
2015	3.83	11.72
2016	2.70	11.50
2017	1.57	11.28

Source: Financial Statements of Insurance Companies

From Table 7.6, the change in the regulation of the insurance companies has had an effect on the trend of the return on equity of the general insurance businesses. This can be deduce from the downward trend in the return on equity from Table 7.6 where the average ROE of both categorised insurance companies started to decline from 2007. This implies that when the activities of the insurance companies were composite, the life insurance business sections were contributing enough revenue to the general profitability of the companies than the general insurance companies. This is because of the seemingly different nature of the operations of the two business activities.

From Table 7.7, the p-values of 0.291 and 0.083 of the long term debt to total capital ratio and total debt to total capital ratio respectively shows that, there is no disparity in the degree of leverage of the insurance companies with age below 20 and those with age above 20 .But short term debt to total capital took an inverse position by establishing a statistically significant difference among the short term debt structure of the two groups of companies having recorded a p-value of 0.037.

Table 7.7: ANOVA table for degree of leverage variables

		Sum of Squares	Df	Mean Square	F	Sig.
STD to TC Ratio	Between Groups	3412.38	1	3408.258	4.442	.037
LTD to TC Ratio	Between Groups	136.19	1	148.039	1.121	.291
TD to TC Ratio	Between Groups	2143.78	1	2233.735	1.034	.083

Source: Financial Statements of Insurance Companies

The import of the results in Table 7.7 is that, insurance companies by the character of their business may not be pleased about the use of long term debt. Therefore when they are newly established, it may like to succumb to the industry practice since there would not be any difference in their preference for long term debt. The same reason can be attached to the use of total debt practice among insurance companies in Ghana. With respect to the short term debt difference between the two groups is as a result of the credit worthiness and the relationship the insurance company might have created overtime.

CHAPTER EIGHT

CORRELATION AND UNIT ROOT TEST ANALYSIS OF THE VARIABLES

Learning Objectives

By the end of this chapter, the reader will be able to:

- *Comprehend the relationship between the independent variables and the dependent variables*
- *Assess the level collinearity between the various variables*
- *Assess the unit root analysis of the variables*

8.0 Introduction

In this chapter, the correlation matrix of the dependent and independent variables of the study is presented and discussed in Table 8.1 while Table 8.2 and 8.3 discusses the panel unit root of the variables to check for their stationary over the period of time of the study since regression will be run with those data and the Hausman Specification test respectively.

8.1 Correlation analysis

The correlation matrix in Table 8.1 examines the possibility of multi-collinearity among the regressors as well as examine whether there is a positive relationship between dependent variables and the independent variables. This is important as it shows whether there is any relationship between the indicators of degree of leverage and financial performance. From Table 8.1, it is observed that return on equity (ROE) is statistically significant negative relationship with all the indicators of degree of leverage which are short term debt (STD), long term debt ratio (LTD) and total debt ratio (TD).

This negative relationship between ROE and the degree of leverage variables imply that when insurance companies contract more debt capital it leads to a reduction in their return on equity. The reason for this situation is because of the bankruptcy cost that company are exposed to whenever they contract debt capital. The bankruptcy cost affects financial performance. The relationship established is similar to the findings of Gatsi (2012).

Table 8.1: Correlations Matrix of the Variable Used in the Study

	ROA	ROE	NPM	STD	LTD	TD	FZ	PG	IF	GDP	EX	Age
ROA	1											
ROE	.785**	1										
NPM	645**	.506**	1									
STD	-.051**	-.149*	.038*	1								
LTD	-.068*	-.141	-.024	-.268**	1							
TD	-.016	-.082*	.024*	.914**	.135	1						
FZ	.025*	-.101*	.074*	-.130	-.016	-.138	1					
PG	.041	-.055	.014	-.006	.056*	-.006	.129	1				
IF	.122*	.061*	.173*	.053	-.032	.036	-.189*	-.26	1			
GDP	-.044	-.041*	.123	-.060	.022	-.050	.206**	.070	-.434**	1		
EX	-.121	-.078*	-.186*	-.199**	-.003	-.214*	.263**	-.04	-.486**	.744**	1	
Age	-.049	-.097	-.046*	-.254**	.198**	-.177*	.293**	.029	-.087	.108	.141	1

** **Significant at the 0.01 level (2-tailed).** * **Significant at the 0.05 level (2-tailed).**
Source: Financial statement of insurance companies

This is because Gatsi (2012) researched on the banking sector using the panel data methodology which was adopted by the current study and also used the same time period coupled with the use of the macro economic variables used in the current study as control variables. ROE is also negatively related to premium growth, firm size, GDP, exchange rate and age of the firms but it should be emphasised that it is the relationships with firm size, GDP and exchange rate that is statistically significant. The statistical significant means as the insurance companies expand in size their financial performance reduces because of the unsustainable cost associated with expansion. This relationship validates the literature of Fu (1997) and Heng and Ong (2011) probably because those studies measured return of equity using the formula adopted for the current study.

In relation to GDP, under normal circumstance as the economy expand, the financial performance of most institutions operating within that economy should expand in the same manner but because insurance is about managing risk, when institutions perform well they tend to institute risk management departments which will seek to implement policies to manage the exposure to operational risks. Therefore those firms usually will not subscribe to insurance policies resulting in the reduction in the financial performance of the insurance companies.

With regards to exchange rate, when customers undertake foreign exchange risk policies with insurance companies and the exchange rate fluctuate over a given period of time, the policy holders turn to resort to insurance companies to mitigate the risk they are exposed to. From this backdrop, since the exchange rate in Ghana has fluctuated over the ten year period under studied, it becomes imperative for an adverse relationship between financial performance and degree of leverage ratios.

Again, from Table 8.1, ROE is positively related to inflation and is statistically significant because as inflation increases and policy holder revalue their asstes, the values of the assets that they have insured also increase therefore the premium to be paid by clients on those assets to the insurance companies increase. The increments are then reflected in the net earnings for the period. ROA is negatively related to STD, LTD and TD recording a statistical significance level showing that all the indicators of degree of leverage of the insurance companies are negatively related to the financial performance indicators such that the gearing levels of the insurance companies are termed to be in an inverse relationship with the asset level of the insurance companies meaning that insurance companies in Ghana do not use their asset to improve financial performance.

With respect to the controlling variables, ROA is positively related to premium growth, firm size and inflation but only the relationship with premium growth is statistically significant. The relationship between firm sizes is positively significant and it is expected because as insurance companies increase in size they are forced to acquire assets to commensurate the requirements for expanding.

On the other hand, ROA recorded a negative relationship with age of the insurance companies, GDP and exchange rate. But the relationship between age of the insurance companies and GDP are statistically insignificant but that of exchange rate is statistically significant since it recorded a p-value of 0.001 probably because if al lot of customers subscribe to exchange rate risk policies and insurance companies are required to redeem such claims, they might be forced to reduce their asset level in order to effectively indemnify such policy holders.

NPM is significantly and positively related to STD and TD while it is significantly and negatively related to LTD. This implies that an increase in the long term debt of the insurance companies in Ghana is likely to decrease the level of net premium margin of the companies while an increase in short term debt in the degree of leverage is mostly like to increase the level of net premium margin of the companies. This findings are in line with the studies of Asimakopoulous, Samitas and Papadogonas (2009) and PretheepKantth (2011) because in both studies the measurement of net profit margin and the degree of leverage variables were what was adopted in the current studies meaning that, irrespective of the area the studies are conducted when the measurement of the variables are the same, it is likely for the same result to be attained irrespective of the fact that it is done on different industries.

This result were expected because net profit margin is measured with earnings before interest and tax meaning that even if the insurance companies increase the capital base of their companies and it result in an increment in premium collection because the interest component is not deducted before that net earnings is used for the computation, the level of net profit margin will continue to increase irrespective of the level of debt contracted by the insurance company. In relation to age and exchange rate used for the study, Table 8.1 shows a statistically significant negative relationship with NPM. NPM had a positive relationship with firm size, premium growth, inflation and GDP. While the relationship with firm size, premium growth and inflation is statistically significant, that of GDP is not statistically significant.

The significant relationship between exchange rate and net profit margin is because when the level of exchange rate increases, the risk averse individuals would prefer to hold foreign exchange rate risk insurance policies which would help mitigate their risks, now as more and more policyholders clinch on the exchange rate risk policies, the premium received by the insurance companies also increases leading to an increase in the net profit margin of the insurance companies. On the other hand, as exchange rate becomes very stable most risk averse investor do not see the need to hold exchange rate risk policies therefore the premium collection level of its customer base reduce leading to a reduction the a reported net profit margin.

In conclusion there seems to be a consistency in the results obtained under both ROE and ROA due to the linearity in the relationship between the financial performance measures because those two financial performance variables are measured based on items on both the income statement and the statement of financial position while that of net profit margin differs from ROA and ROE because the measurement of NPM is based on only income statement items.

8.2 Unit root analysis

In a regression analysis, since a linear relationship is expected to be established between the variables of concern, there is the need for a unit root test to be conducted to establish whether the variables used in the study are stationary or not stationary. For this reason since the current study is based on panel regression, there is the need for a panel unit root tests to be designed to test the null hypothesis of a unit root for each individual series in a panel.

Table 8.2: Panel Unit Root

Variable Method	Statistic	Prob.**	Order
D(GDP) Levin, Lin & Chu t*	-10.7421	0.0000	1
D(EX) Levin, Lin & Chu t*	4.10179	0.0000	1
IF Levin, Lin & Chu t*	-6.76524	0.0000	0
D(FS) Levin, Lin & Chu t*	-3.91729	0.0000	1
PG Levin, Lin & Chu t*	-6.36484	0.0000	0
STD Levin, Lin & Chu t*	-4.66306	0.0000	0
LTD Levin, Lin & Chu t*	-4.51081	0.0000	0
TD Levin, Lin & Chu t*	-7.48384	0.0000	0
ROA Levin, Lin & Chu t*	-1.61991	0.0526	0
ROE Levin, Lin & Chu t*	-5.21883	0.0000	0
NPM Levin, Lin & Chu t*	-4.91373	0.0000	0

Source: Financial Statements of Insurance Companies

From Table 8.2, the Levin, Lin, and Chu (2002) panel unit root is used to analysis the stationary of the variables to be used in the study and it hypothesis a null hypothesis of a data assuming a common stationary. This model was used because, Westerlund and Breitung (2009) indicated that the local power of the Levin, Lin, and Chu (2002) test is greater than that of the Im, Pesaran, and Shin (2003) test, which is based on a less restrictive alternative, also when not all individual series are stationary

The stationary test result of the time series variables using the Levin, Lin, and Chu unit root test approach as shown in Table 8.2, GDP, exchange rate and firm size had their unit roots at lag 1 with inflation, premium growth, short term debt to total capital ratio, long term debt to total capital ratio, total debt to total capital ratio return on asset and return on equity showing its stationary at the difference zero having recorded a p-value of less than 0.05.

Since, the incorporated variables in this study are not of the same order of stationary, the researcher assumed the same level of stability in the data distribution pattern that is to say, the same order of stationary for the subsequent tests. Otherwise, the long-run relationship would not be established excluding the short-run analysis which does not require the same order of integration.

8.3 The Hausman specification test

The Hausman specification test is a test carried out on the panel data prior to running a panel data regression to establish whether the researcher should choose the fixed effects or the random effects in the model estimation. The random effects model assumes that there is no correlation between the group specific random effects and the regressors. However, the fixed effects model does not make such assumption and the possibility remains that the assumption of zero correlation in random effects model is not feasible. As a rule of thumb, if carried out and the probability value is less than 0.05 (i.e., $p < 0.05$) then there is a correlation between the error terms and the explanatory variables so the fixed effects is adopted in the model estimation otherwise the random effects is an inefficient estimator of the parameters under investigation. Table 8.3 above shows the results of the Hausman specification tests.

Degree of Leverage: Empirical analysis from the insurance sector

Table 8.3: Hausman specification test

Variables	Chi–Square Statistic	P-Values
ROE= STD+SIZE+PG+AGE+INF+GDP+ER	21.6889	0.0000
ROE= LTD+SIZE+PG+AGE+INF+GDP+ER	29.1672	0.0000
ROE= TD+SIZE+PG+AGE+INF+GDP+ER	22.8967	0.0001
ROA= STD+SIZE+PG+AGE+INF+GDP+ER	19.6572	0.0003
ROA= LTD+SIZE+PG+AGE+INF+GDP+ER	35.5766	0.0000
ROA= TD+SIZE+PG+AGE+INF+GDP+ER	36.8276	0.0000
NPM= STD+SIZE+PG+AGE+INF+GDP+ER	23.5778	0.0001
NPM= LTD+SIZE+PG+AGE+INF+GDP+ER	22.6785	0.0001
NPM= TD+SIZE+PG+AGE+INF+GDP+ER	18.3425	0.0004

Source: Financial Statements of Insurance Companies

Where ROE represents returns on equity, ROA represents return on asset, NPM represents net profit margin, STD represents Short Term Debts to capital ratio, LTD represents Long Term Debts to capital ratio, TD represents Total Debt to capital ratio, SZ represents Firm Size for firm, PG represents premium growth, AGE represent the difference between the established year and the year under observation, IF represent inflation GDP represent gross domestic product and EX represent exchange rate. From Table 8.3, the Hausman specification test, it can be observed that all the probability values in the nine models are below 0.05. This implies that, the random effects model should be rejected and thus the analysis is based on the fixed effects estimates, therefore it is far-sighted to use fixed effects as this approach produces a more resourceful parameter estimates. Reimoo (2008) also compared fixed effects model with the random effects model and based their results on fixed effects model on the basis of Hausman specification test.

CHAPTER NINE

REGRESSION RESULTS AND DISCUSSION

Learning Objectives

By the end of this chapter, the reader will be able to comprehend the influence of:

- *Long term debt on the financial performance of insurance companies*
- *short term debt on the financial performance of insurance companies*
- *total debt on the financial performance of insurance companies*
- *selected macroeconomic indicators on the financial performance of insurance companies*

9.1 Panel regression results

In this subsection, the various panel data regressions are discussed. Regression analysis was used to examine the relationship between degree of leverage and financial performance of insurance companies in Ghana, which is measured by returns on equity (ROE), returns on asset (ROA) and net profit margin (NPM). From Table 9.1, ROA has statistically significant negatively relationship with STD, LTD and TD this is because, the financial performance ratios indicated a p-value less than 0.05 meaning they are all significant at 5 percent. But the coefficient for LTD shows a much larger negative relationship indicating that if insurance companies continue to increase their long term debt component of their degree of leverage, it would lead to a decrease in the level of ROA of the insurance companies and this might be due to the quantum of the interest payment on the long term debt contracted by the insurance companies.

Table 9.1: Regression for return on asset as dependent variable

Variables	Profitability: ROA					
	STD		LTD		TD	
	Coef.	Sig.	Coef.	Sig.	Coef.	Sig.
Constant	40.145**	0.004	45.111**	0.002	41.669**	0.009
Firm Size	0.747*	0.035	0.723*	0.036	0.734*	0.037
Age	-0.439	0.258	-0.567	0.149	-0.523	0.207
Premium Growth	0.003	0.903	-0.026	0.308	0.021	0.938
STD	-0.025*	0.028				
LTD			-0.205*	0.038		
TD					-0.035*	0.026
R-squared	0.609		0.613		0.616	
Adjusted R^2	0.527		0.533		0.536	
F – Statistic	7.459		7.599		7.697	
Prob.(F-stats)	0.000**		0.000**		0.000**	
Durbin-Wastson	1.244		1.200		1.205	

*Significant level at 5% ** Significance at 1%
Source: Financial Statements of Insurance Companies

The significance at 5 percent and 1 percent means that the null hypothesis will be accepted if the null hypothesis is below 5 percent. With respect to the controlling variables, firm size, premium growth, and inflation indicated a positive relationship on ROA but out of these variables, firm size and inflation showed a statistically significant relationship across all the degree of leverage variables hence the need for much attention to be given to these variables.

This implies that insurance companies with larger size influence the level of the ROA partly because those insurance firms might have the required assets that would facilitates their operations in terms having the required experienced and well-motivated staffs as well as technological facilities in drawing up attractive insurance policies that would increase their client base. Obviously as more clients subscribe to insurance policies, the premiums that an insurance companies would receive in a given period increases leading to an increase in the financial performance indicators.

Inflation also causes ROA to increase because when there is a general increase in the price in an economy; the import is that, over a given period of time, the values of items both tangible and intangible would increase in value and so even if the rate of premium charged by insurance companies remains stable, the increment in the value of asset that has been revalued by the customers would cause premium to be received by the insurance companies to also increase. So if by the end of the period the request of claim payment falls, it implies that all thing being equal the financial performance of the insurance companies would also increase.

This is consistent with the findings of by Abor and Beikpe (2009) and Symeou (2008) although both studies were not specifically based on the insurance sector. The similarity in the findings with the work by Abor and Beikpe (2009) is as a result of the fact that their study was based on the Ghanaian economy as well as the use of the panel data methodology. Their study also used the degree of leverage measurements used in the current study. With respect to the study by Symeou (2008), the similarity stems from the fact that, Symeou's study compared firm size and inflation to performance and also a critical review of the study found that ROA was used as the financial performance indicator and firm size was measured just as used the measurement adopted in the current study.

It is worth nothing that, the age of the insurance companies indicated a negative relationship across the various degree of leverage indicators but the relationship is not statistically significant hence there no relationship between the age of the insurance companies and ROA as a financial performance indicator .The R-squared form Table 9.1 indicates that the independent variables explain 61 percent of the relationship between the dependent variables. On the other hand the adjusted R squared shows a much lower percentage of about 54 percent because of the introduction of a larger number of controlling variable. The Durbin-Watson statistic (DW) measures the serial correlation in the residuals. As a rule of thumb, if the DW is less than 2, there is an evidence of positive serial correlation. The DW statistic from Table 9.1 shows a coefficient of 1.2, indicating the presence of serial correlation in the residuals.

Table 9.2: Regression for Return on equity as dependent variable

Variables	Profitability: ROE					
	STD		LTD		TD	
	Coef.	Sig.	Coef.	Sig.	Coef.	Sig.
Constant	8.347**	0.013	4.431**	0.132	10.037**	0.003
Firm Size	-0.016	0.055	-0.130**	0.014	-0.012*	0.042
Age	-0.092	0.385	0.021	0.833	-0.127	0.214
Premium Growth	-0.004	0.919	-0.002	0.805	-0.004	0.951
STD	-0.026*	0.036				
LTD			-0.039	0.138		
TD					-0.038**	0.002
R-squared	0.628		0.581		0.660	
Adjusted R²	0.553		0.497		0.592	
F – Statistic	8.357		6.877		9.636	
Prob.(F-stats)	0.000**		0.000**		0.000**	
Durbin-Waston	1.812		1.844		1.804	

*Significant level at 5% ** Significance at 1%
Source: Financial Statements of Insurance Companies

Degree of Leverage: Empirical analysis from the insurance sector

Table 9.2 indicates that, return on equity (ROE) is significantly and negatively related to STD and TD with p-values of 0.0356 and 0.0019 respectively. This means the relationship is significant at 5 percent but TD showed a much higher coefficient meaning that if the insurance companies wants to increase their ROE values they would have to reduce the amount of debt in their degree of leverage. Firm size and premium growth are positively related with ROE with significant p-values with the exception of premium growth which showed a p-valve greater than 5 percent. This finding is similar to the outcomes by fu (1997), Seed (2010) and Ahmad, Naveed and Zulfquar (2011). The reason why the result seems to be in line the study by Ahmad et al (2011) is that, their study concentrated on the insurance sector just as the current work but the study was done in the Pakistan economy.

Apart from that the study used a similar methodology and estimated the firm size and premium growth just as the current study estimated those variables. With respect to the study by Fu (1997), the similarity between that study and the current study is as a result of method of estimation both studies adopted and considering the fact that the degree of leverage measures were also similar.

To add to the above, because debt negatively influence returns on equity significantly in the insurance of Ghana, the evidence in is that, the levels of retained earnings of insurance companies will continue to ascend in the books of most insurance thus depriving shareholders of dividends at least in the short-run. This assertion confirms statistics in the National insurance commission (NIC) Report for 2011 where it was found that the industry average return on equity for 2010 and 2011 was 7 percent and 3 percent respectively. Both were below 10 percent meaning that if the investor had invested in Treasury bills which are considered to be risk free in those periods, that investor would have earned a much higher return because the Treasury bill rate for 2010 and 2011 were 12 percent and 18 percent respectively (Ghana Statistical Service Report, 2011).

Another reason for the adverse relation of debt (be it short-term, long-term, and total) in influencing returns on equity is as a result of increasing costs of doing the business of insurance in emerging economies including Ghana. The resultant effect of this is that, all thing being equal, it reduces profits which could have gone to shareholders. These costs include increasing employee salaries, investments in information technology, acquisition and maintenance of chauffeured premises. This result is consistent with the study by Abor (2008), Akoto and Gatsi (2010), because each these studies were conducted on the financial sectors on the Ghanaian economy. Najjar and Petrov (2011) also confirmed this finding partly because their studies covered the insurance industry though that study was based on the Bahraini economy.

The controlling variables such as firm size and premium growth indicated a negative relationship with ROE, but none of the coefficients showed a statistical significance This outcome evidences the studies of Papadogonas and Samitas (2009) whose study also established a negative relationship between profitability and return on equity. From the Table 9.2 the R-squared which measures the extent to which the explanatory variables explain the variations in the ROE is about 66 percent. Again from the same table the Durbin-Watson Statistic (D-W Statistic) revealed that the problem of autocorrelation of the errors terms which is sometimes a challenge in panel data methodology is not serious in the ROE regression estimates because of the average coefficient of 1.8 which was identified in Table 9.2.

The F-test which shows the global usefulness of the model indicated an appreciable goodness of fit. In other words, the F-statistics prove the validity of the estimated models is statistically significant at 1 percent as shown by the F-probabilities. The constant term indicates the returns on equity levels if all the explanatory variables are put to zero. It is significant at about 0.35 percent and shows that other factors which equally impact on returns on equity have not been captured in the model.

From Table 9.3, the regression estimates using net profit margin as the main dependent variable showed the highest R squared of about 83 percent meaning that, the variables used in the study as regressors largely explains the variation in NPM than any of the financial performance indicators. Unlike the other financial performance used by the researcher, NPM showed a positive significant relationship with STD and TD with a p-valve of 2.6 percent and 4.6 percent respectively while LTD showed an insignificant negative relationship with NPM. But this outcome is in consonance with Peterson and Rajan (1994) El-Wahid and Singapurwoko (2011) because of the similarity in the measurement of net profit margin.

Table 9.3: Regression for net profit margin as dependent variable

Variables	Profitability: NPM					
	STD		LTD		TD	
	Coef.	Sig.	Coef.	Sig.	Coef.	Sig.
Constant	9.347**	0.000	7.431**	0.000	9.811**	0.000
Firm Size	3.190*	0.032	3.204*	0.037	3.094*	0.037
Age	-1.242**	0.010	-1.409**	0.004	-1.270**	0.011
Premium Growth	0.043	0.172	0.045	0.168	0.044	0.176
STD	0.031**	0.026				
LTD			-0.022	0.081		
TD					0.027**	0.045
R-squared	0.828		0.826		0.828	
Adjusted R^2	0.794		0.791		0.793	
F – Statistic	23.892		23.606		23.792	
Prob.(F-stas)	0.000**		0.000**		0.000**	
Durbin-Waston	1.512		1.519		1.504	

*Significant level at 5% ** Significance at 1%
Source: Financial Statements of Insurance Companies

Age, firm size and premium growth which are industry specific indicators indicated a negative relationship with NPM. Age and firm size showed a statistically significant and needs to be considered relevant. This implies that, the ages of the insurance companies and their size influence their NPM in an adverse such that when the firms' age and size increases their NPM fall. The reason could be attributed to the immerse competition new insurance companies bring into the industry. This outcome is in consonance with Dong (2011), in a study on foreign exchange rate and degree of leverage decision partly because his study was based on a small economy synonymous to the economy of Ghana

Furthermore from the same table the Durbin-Watson Statistic (D-W Statistic) shows that the problem of auto correlation is not serious with respect to NPM with an average value of 1.5. Also the F-statistics and the F-test prove the validity of the estimated models which are statistically significant at one percent as shown by the F-probabilities. The constant term indicates the returns on equity levels if all the explanatory variables are put to zero. It is significant at about 0.00 percent and shows that other factors which equally impact on returns on equity have not been captured in the model.

9.2 Regression for Performance Variables and Macroeconomic indicators

This section of the chapter focuses on the effect of the three dominant macroeconomic indicators on the financial performance of the insurance companies. From table 9.4, it is worth nothing that, exchange rate and GDP indicated a negative relationship across the various financial performance indicators but in the case of GDP none the relationship is statistically significant hence there no relationship between the GDP and the financial performance indicators .

Table 9.4. Regression for Performance Variables and Macroeconomic indicators

Variables	ROA		ROE		NPM	
	Coeff	Sig.	Coeff.	Sig.	Coeff.	Sig
Constant	-0.032	0.466	-0.733	0.110	0.963	0.003
GDP	-0.068	0.494	-0.012	0.901	-0.049	0.912
Exchange Rate	-2.465*	0.023	-2.431*	0.031	-2.295*	0.026
Inflation Rate	-0.017**	0.014	0.099**	0.014	0.094*	0.018
R-squared	0.699		0.654		0.620	
Adjusted R²	0.511		0.546		0.549	
F – Statistic	3.185		2.657		1.548	
Prob.(F-stas)	0.000**		0.000**		0.000**	
Durbin-Waston	2.838		2.891		2.931	

*Significant level at 5% ** Significance at 1%

On the other hand, only the coefficients of exchange rate showed a statistical significance with a p-value 0.023, 0.031 and 0.026 for ROA, ROE and NPM respectively meaning that an increase in the depreciation of the Ghanaian currency is against other currencies affect the financial performance of the insurance companies simply because those policyholders who might have insured against exchange rate risk; resort to the insurance companies for their claims which will in turn reduce the proceeds used to compute the performance of the insurance companies. This outcome evidences the studies of Gatsi and Gadzo (2013) whose study also established a negative relationship between profitability and exchange rate. With respect to inflation, the results in Table 9.4 showed a statistically positive relationship with NPM and ROE implying that a general increase in the NPM and ROE when the level of inflation reduces. The results also indicated a statistically negative relationship between inflation and ROA of the insurance companies.

From the Table 9.4 the R-squared which measures the extent to which the explanatory variables explain the variations in the ROA, ROE and NPM is 69%, 65% and 62% respectively. Again from the same table the Durbin-Watson Statistic (D-W Statistic) revealed that the problem of autocorrelation of the errors terms which is sometimes a challenge in panel data methodology is not serious in the ROE regression estimates because of the average coefficient of 1.8 which was identified in Table 9.2.

9.3 Research hypothesis testing

The hypothesis was tested using the p – values of the relationships that were established in the regression results in Table 9.2. This is because return on equity is used to measure financial performance because of the usage of the formula inculcated return on asset in its estimation which was used in estimating the return on equity as explained in chapter three. The hypothesis are tested in three main categories thus in terms of degree of leverage variables, macroeconomic variables and the firm specific variables

9.3.1 Hypothesis formulated for the degree of leverage variables

From Table 9.2 above results hypothesis 1, 2 and 3 can be addressed. The hypotheses are;

H1: Financial performance has a relationship with short –term debt ratio of insurance companies in Ghana.
H2: Financial performance has a relationship with long –term debt ratio of insurance companies in Ghana.
H3: Financial performance of has a relationship with total debt ratio of insurance companies in Ghana.

From Table 9.2, the p-value for the short – term debt ratio and ROE is 0.0356. This is below the bench mark alpha of 0.05, thus the null hypothesis is rejected. This is because there is a relationship between financial performance and short term debt ratio but the relationship is a negative one which implies that the financial performances of the insurance companies are inversely associated to the short term debt components of their capital. This result can be attributed to the reason that the return of equity representing financial performance as measured in the study considered the return on asset as part of its estimation.

This explanation therefore means that, the bankruptcy cost that the company will be exposed to will lead to the fall in the financial performance of insurance companies because of the impact it would have on the performance level of the company. This finding is not in consonance with the free cash flow theory and the studies by Afrasibishani, Ahmadinia and Hesami (2012) simply because, the assumptions' upon which those studies were done can are not the same in the case of the economy of Ghana.

With respect to hypothesis 2, because the p –value ($p>0.138$) is greater than the acceptable level of 5 percent from Table 8.1, so the null hypothesis is accepted because the negative relationship reported is not significant. Therefore, there is no relationship between financial performance and long term debt ratio. This confirms the assertion of M&M propositions II that the degree of leverage of companies has no relationship with the value of the firm.

For hypothesis 3, because the relationship between total debt ratio and ROE is significant at 0.002, financial performance has no relationship with total debt ratio of insurance companies in Ghana is rejected. The relationship established by the study is a negative one such that whenever insurance companies in Ghana increase their total debt component in their degree of leverage, their financial performance decreases. The reason for the negative relationship comes from the pecking order theory and a meaning can be provided that because of the agency and bankruptcy cost might have caused this relationship simply because as insurance companies incur more costs those costs eventually reduce their financial performance.

9.3.2 Hypothesis formulated for the macroeconomic

At this point, the hypothesis stated in relation to macroeconomic variables can be addressed. The hypotheses are;

H4: Financial performance of insurance companies has a relationship with the rate of inflation
H5: Financial performance of insurance companies has a relationship with gross domestic product
H6: Financial performance of insurance companies has a relationship with exchange rate

From Table 9.4, the null hypothesis 4 is rejected and the alternate hypothesis is accepted because inflation establishes a relationship with the financial performance of insurance companies in Ghana at a significant level of 5 percent. It is imperative to mention that, the relationship established with all the financial performance indicators are positive ones with a p – value of 0.017 which is less than 0.05 ($P<0.05$). Indicating that, indeed the level of inflation directly influences the pattern of financial performance in the insurance sector of Ghana.

The reason for this relationship can be explained that as inflation increases the general price level in the economy also increases, culminating into the values of the assets insured by policy holders also increasing leading to an increase in the premiums collection by the insurance companies on their insurance policies. It be emphasised that even if the premium rate remains the same, the increment in the values of assets would lead to an increase in the premiums to be collected. This will eventually lead to an increment profits by the insurance companies which invariably affects their financial performance.

Again, hypothesis 5 which has a hypothesis that financial performance of insurance companies has a relationship with gross domestic product, is not accepted based on the average p-values of 0.710 which is greater than the acceptable value of 0.05 thus (p>0.05). Therefore, is no relationship established between financial performance and gross domestic product, the alternate hypothesis is rejected because of the statistically insignificant nature of the relationship established.

The import of this finding is that whether the gross domestic product of Ghana increases or decrease, it has no effect on the financial performance of the insurance sector. The reason for this is that insurance companies by their nature, are risk mitigating agents so whether the amount of goods and service produced by a given economy increases or not, it does not in any way affect the risks that insurance companies mitigate. This finding is not in consonance with the study by Lara and Mesquita (2002) because their study was conducted on the Brazilian economy whose gross domestic product is different from that of Ghana.

Unlike the other macroeconomic variables whose alternate hypotheses have been rejected, exchange rate from all the panel regression tables establishes a negative relationship with the financial performance indicators with an average p-value of 0.026 which is less than the acceptable range hence hypothesis 6 is rejected while its alternate hypothesis is accepted meaning that, there is a relationship between the financial performance of insurance companies and exchange rate but the relationship is a negative one meaning that, the level of exchange rate adversely affects the financial performance of insurance companies in Ghana.

This means that insurance companies should be mindful of accepting exchange rate risk policies from clients as it might negatively affect its cash flows negatively due to the recurrent payment of claim to their clients on exchange rate issues

9.3.3 Hypothesis formulated for the firm specific variables

The hypothesis of the firm specific variables can be addressed from this point. These hypotheses are stated as;

H7: Financial performance of insurance companies has a relationship with their size
H8: Financial performance of insurance companies has a relationship with their premium growth
H9: Financial performance of insurance companies has a relationship with their age

From Table 9.2, the p-value for the firm size and the financial performance indicator revealed a value of 0.042 this is below the bench mark alpha of 0.05 and because it has established a negative relationship, the null hypothesis is rejected based on the premises of the negative relationship with financial performance. The negative relationship between insurance size and financial performance suggests that larger insurance companies tend to exhibit lower margins and is consistent with models that emphasize the negative role of size from scale inefficiencies. This agrees with previous empirical works of Ishfaq, Naveed and Zulfquar (2010) and Gatsi (2012). Therefore, the evidence from this study solidifies the reason of rejecting the null hypothesis that insurance companies' size and financial performance are not negatively related in the insurance sector of Ghana.

With respect to the null hypothesis 8, it is accepted on the premises that, though the coefficient from the above table indicates a negative relationship, the null hypothesis is accepted because of an average p-value of 0.9004 which is greater than 0.05 (P>0.05) meaning that there is no relationship between the premium growth and financial performance of insurance companies. In the literature, insurance companies generally would increase their profits as the level of premium grows thus as the level of premium grows it results to a higher financial performance of the insurance companies.

According to this school of thought, there exist a positive relationship between premium growth and financial performance. In this study, there is no relationship between premium growth and financial performance. This means that premium growth is less important in determining insurance companies' financial performance in Ghana. The possible reason for this finding is that, premium can attain an all time growth but if the claims by policy holders in a given year are high, the meaning is that most of the premiums collected would be used in indemnifying clients who have been exposed to risk.

On the other hand if premium collection does not increase in a given period, there could be no claims from clients therefore the financial performance of insurance companies would remain the same over a given period. The current study is not in consonance with the research by Abor (2008) who found a significant positive relationship between growth in Ghanaian in firms and their financial performance but his studies was based on Small and Medium scale business, quoted firms and unquoted firms.

The reason for the difference is that insurance companies were not considered in the study. But the current study is in consonance with the findings by Gatsi (2012) due to the fact that his study was conducted on the banking sector of Ghana which is also part of the financial sector. Apart from that Gatsi (2012) study cover the time frame of ten years which the current study also covered.

Finally, from Table 9.2, the coefficients of the financial performance indicator which is return on equity revealed a relationship with the age of the insurance companies, but though this assertion is in consonance with the alternate hypothesis, that there is a relationship between financial performance and the age of insurance companies in Ghana, the null hypothesis accepted based on the premises that the p – value of 0.214 is way above the benchmark limit of 0.05. This implies that irrespective of the age of the insurance companies in Ghana, the company can either improve on their financial performance or not.

CHAPTER TEN

SUMMARY, CONCLUSION AND RECOMMENDATIONS

Learning Objectives

By the of end of this chapter, the reader will be able to;

- *Analysis of the effect of leverage on the performance of insurance companies in Ghana*
- *Understand policies to be implemented by regulatory bodies on how effective leverage of insurance companies can be managed to yield the needed results*

10.1 Introduction

The role that insurance companies play in the economic development of every country cannot be overemphasised. Principally, insurance companies serve as intermediaries who mediate between the surplus and deficit spending units as well as mitigating the business risk, which are exposed to the individual, the business sector as well as the government as a whole by taking premiums from those who patronise their product and indemnify them whenever they are exposed to the risks.

One principal decision managers of insurance companies usually undertake for the survival of their company is the mix of capital they use in their operations. This option is indispensable for the determination of the financial performance of the insurance companies. This implies that insurance companies that are able to make their financing decision far-sightedly would have a cut-throat in the industry and thus result in above average financial performance relative to the insurance industry, However, it is vital to mention that this strategic decision can only be shrewdly taken if management of insurance companies know how debt policy influences their financial performance.

10.2 Summary

This current study investigated the relationship between degree of leverage and financial performance of insurance companies in Ghana. The objectives of the study was to determine the nature of degree of leverage practice among insurance companies in Ghana and to examine the relation between their degree of leverage and their financial performance, firms specific variables and macroeconomic variable. The study covered 18 insurance companies over the period 2002-2017. Panel data methodology was adopted and the major findings of the study are summarized below:

First of all, it was identified that 60.53 percent of the total capital of insurance companies in Ghana is made up of debt. Of this, 50.86 percent represent short-term debts while 9.76 percent is made up of long-term debts. This is consistent with the assertion of Najjar and Petrov, (2011) that insurance companies debt level are slightly above average and also highlights the importance of short-term debts over long-term debts in financing insurance business in Ghana. This finding agrees with previous studies such as (Ahmad, Naveed, and Zulfquar, 2010) in stressing the importance of short-term debt in financing insurance companies in Ghana.

The study also revealed that there are no significant differences among the insurance companies with respect to the financial performance indicators as well as their degree of leverage after an analysis of variance had been conducted between insurance companies which had an average age below and above twenty during the period understudy. It was also determined from the results that majority of the dependent and the main independent variable were stationary as compared to the controlling variable which stationary at the first difference.

Short-term debt, long-term debt, and total debt were found to be negatively significant at 3 percent, 4 percent, and 4 percent respectively in determining financial performance in the insurance sector of Ghana. This means that debts that are contracted by insurance companies do not necessarily translate into enhancing financial performance in the insurance industry in Ghana. One reason is the increasing cost of debt in the economy of Ghana which is consequently driving down financial performance in various sectors of the economy.

Another reason is the high premium charges by the insurance sector of Ghana which is deterring many business and households from acquiring insurance products. It is crucial to note that when debts capital are received by insurance companies and they are not able to transform them into insurance products for clients, it implies that these debts would not in any way influence financial performance. It is also important to note that higher premium charges by the insurance companies before insurance policies are contracted by the public is one of the key issues that is impeding the insurance penetration rate in Ghana.

When this happens the general public is unmotivated to have insurance policies thus making debts contracted to finance insurance activities insignificant in determining financial performance of the insurance companies. Last but not least, factors that explains why debt is not important in determining return on asset and returns on equity in the insurance sector of Ghana is increased competition which is lowering policy takers base of each insurance company hence their returns.

With regards to the relationship between short-term debt and net premium margin, the regression result indicated a significantly positive association. This means that as short-term debts increase in the insurance sector of Ghana, net profit margin increases. The main reason for this phenomenon is the tax shield attribute of debt which was discussed in the review of literature. And it is so because of net profit margin was computed using before interest and tax, the interest component paid on debt does not affect the amount of net profit.

In the study, long-term debt is negative but insignificant in determining net profit margin in the insurance sector of Ghana. This is not staggering since companies use very low levels of long-term debt in their operations as depicted into the descriptive statistic. Another reason is that, the capital market, where insurance companies can access long-term debt is not developed in Ghana. Total debt is significant and positively related to net profit margin in the study.

This means that as leverage increases in the insurance sector of Ghana, financial performance expressed as net profit margin increases. This finding suggests that insurance companies with high financial performance in Ghana use more debt or they depend more on external funds rather than internally generated as their main financing option. This result is consistent with Rajan and Zingales (1994) and El-Wahid and Singapurwoko (2011) and does not support the pecking order theory of firm financing.

The results of this study has revealed that insurance companies size which is defined as the logarithm of total assets is significant and positively related to both returns on equity and return on asset and net profit margin in the insurance sector of Ghana. This means that insurance companies' size is very important in determining their financial performance in Ghana. However, what is important for us to note is that as insurance size increases their financial performance also increases in Ghana and when the insurance size decrease, their financial performance also reduces.

This significant negative relationship between insurance size and financial performance suggests that larger banks tend to exhibit higher margins and is consistent with models that emphasize the positive role of size from scale inefficiencies. This disagrees with previous empirical works such as Gatsi (2012) and Ishfaq, Naveed and Zulfquar (2010). Furthermore, there exists a negative and statistically insignificant relationship between age of the insurance companies and all the financial performance indicators in the insurance sector of Ghana.

Theoretically, insurance companies increase their financial performance as they age due to the learning curve experience. The finding suggests that age of insurance companies is not important in determining insurance companies profit in Ghana. What is significant however, is as the companies' increases in age; their financial performance also reduces and is in line with the theoretical prediction. Some earlier studies also established this position, for example (Ahmad, Naveed & Zulfquar, 2011).

Also, the study found a positive and statistically insignificant relationship between the premium growth and financial performance of insurance companies in Ghana. This means that premium growth is less important in determining insurance companies' financial performance in Ghana. But what is significant for the findings to acknowledge is that as premium growth increases in the insurance sector in Ghana, financial performance also increases and is in line with the theoretical prediction.

Inflation which is one of the significant macroeconomic variables and transcend across all facet of the economy was found to have positive influence on the financial performance of insurance companies in Ghana and was statistical significant. This implies that as inflation increases and policy holders should revalue their assets, insurance companies' collect more premium charges which in turn lead to an increment in the financial performance of the insurance companies.

Unlike inflation, exchange rate revealed a significantly negative relationship with financial performance of insurance companies in Ghana. This implies that exchange rate adversely affects the financial performance of insurance companies in Ghana hence insurance companies should be mindful of accepting exchange rate risk as it might negatively affect its cash flows negatively due to the recurrent payment of claim to their clients on exchange rate issues. This outcome is in consonance with Dong (2011). Finally GDP showed an insignificant negative relationship with the financial performance of the insurance companies in Ghana.

10.3 Conclusions

There is a significant difference in the degree of leverage practices of insurance companies whose average age is below 20 and the insurance companies whose average age is above 20 as well as their financial performance. Short-term debts, long term debts, and total debt are negatively significant in determining returns on equity (ROE) and Return on asset (ROA) in the insurance sector of Ghana.

This has been attributed to increased cost of debt in the type of debts that are contracted by insurance companies in Ghana coupled with the inefficiency in transforming debts into affordable insurance policy that would attract the public. In relation to, firm specific variables like premium growth and size of the insurance companies' they influences financial performance measured as returns on equity, return on asset (ROA) and net profit margin (NPM) positively.

This significant positive relationship between insurance companies size and profitability suggests that larger insurance companies tend to exhibit higher margins and is consistent with models that emphasize the positive role of size from scale inefficiencies while that of premium growth suggests that growth in premium is crucial in determining insurance companies financial performance in Ghana such that when it increases, performance also increase. This result is in line with the theoretical prediction that as the insurance industry increases efforts to increase the penetration rate; there is the likelihood that they will increase their financial performance.

In relation to the macro economic variables which were used as controlling variables in the study, inflation rate influences the financial performance of the insurance companies positively such that when the level of inflation raises their performance level also increase therefore insurance companies needs to draft strategies whenever there are projections of increases in the level of inflation in the future to improve on their financial performance. The other macro-economic variables such as exchange rate and GDP growth also indicated an adverse influence on the financial performance hence insurance companies should be mindful especially in the case of exchange rate not to draft a lot of insurance policies on exchange rate risks since it would adversely reduce their financial performance.

The study also found that profitable insurance companies in Ghana use less debt and depend more on internal sources of financing thus supporting the pecking order theory. In addition to the above, the study has also revealed that long-term debt is not significant in explaining financial performance measured as net profit margin in the insurance sector of Ghana. This is probably due to the absence of a well-developed capital market in Ghana, where insurance companies can raise enough long-term debt.

10.4 Recommendations

The conclusions made from this research have bearings on the academic world, the business or enterprise players particularly the professionals involved in the formulation of financial policies in the insurance industry and for policy makers.

In terms of the academia, this study had added to the plethora of empirical evidence that the Modigliani and Millar Propositions were not applicable in the practical insurance sector in the Ghanaian context. Therefore, this study strengthened the view kept by many financial experts that the Modigliani and Miller Propositions, which challenged that degree of leverage has no impact on a firm's value, was not applicable in an imperfect market with corporate taxes or any costs associated with trading securities.

In short, the major recommendation for academicians is that the use of the Modigliani and Millar Proposition in the context of insurance companies in Ghana should be limited to conditions where company taxes could be held nonexistent. Rather much attention should be given the static trade-off theories, the pecking order and the free cash flow theories since the current study reveals consistency with those theories.

For practitioners, this study strongly recommends that insurance companies should strive towards achieving an optimal degree of leverage.

1. Financial controllers, of insurance companies in particular, should try to adjust and readjust the degree of leverage of their companies in order to reach optimally. If the general practise was to be taken as a guide, insurance companies should keep the total debt to equity at very low between the two sources of funding.
2. This study also recommends that care has to be taken when insurance companies increase their liabilities. As high interest charges would adversely affect their financial performance, managers must always be alert on the level of debt to equity so as not to affect profitability negatively.
3. Insurance companies in Ghana must not be only interested in mobilising debt finance for their companies but must also be concerned with utilising these debts effectively and efficiently. To achieve this, the insurance companies must use these funds to develop attractive insurance policies for the public to patronise.
4. Further, insurance companies policy that aims at always charging higher premiums should be reviewed to the public into insurance. This is not to say that the premiums charged on each insurance policy must not be effectively appraised.

Policy makers have an interest in promoting the insurance sector by making it stable and efficient in order to increase the penetration rate and also the intermediation role of insurance. A prerequisite to formulating effective insurance policies to some extent depends on the understanding of how degree of leverage influences the profitability of insurance. To add to the above, it is often the desire of top management of every insurance company to make prudent financing decision in order to remain financially sound and competitive. A condition to achieve this also to some extent, needs a sound knowledge of how degree of leverage influences financial performance of insurance companies.

Based on the findings of the study, the following is recommended for policy makers in Ghana.

1. Efforts must also be geared towards prudent cutting down of costs of debt and other ancillary cost in the insurance sector in Ghana.
2. The government, through Bank of Ghana, must develop our bond market so that insurance companies can raise a lot of long-term debt which they need to meet their short to medium term loan operations.
3. Reduce the exchange rate policies to one when the exchange rate is unfavourable to Ghana to avoid making losses.

REFERENCES

Abor, J. (2008). Determinants of the degree of leverage of Ghanaian firms. *African Economic Research Consortium, Research paper* No. 176, Nairobi.

Abor, J., & Biekpe, N. (2005). What determines the degree of leverage of listed firms in Ghana? *African Finance Journal*, 7 (1), 37-48.

Abor, J., & Biekpe, N. (2009). How do we explain the degree of leverage of SMEs in sub Saharan Africa? Evidence from Ghana, *Journal of Economic Studies*, 36(1), 83-97.

Abu-Rub, N (2012). Degree of leverage and firm performance: Evidence from Palestine stock exchange. *Euro Journals,* 23 (3), 214-356.

Ahmad, U., Naveed, A. & Zulfqar, A. (2010). Determinants of performance: A case of life insurance sector of Pakistan. *International Research Journal of Finance and Economics*, 61 (2), 123 – 128

Ahmadinia, H., Afrasiabishani, J., & Hesami, E. (2012). A comprehensive review on degree of leverage theories. *The Romanian Economic Journal*, 45 (4). 3-26.

Akoto, R. K., & Gatsi, J.G. (2010). Degree of leverage and profitability in Ghanaian Banks. *Social Science Research Net Work.* Retrieved from www.ssrn.com

Al-Bashs, R., & Sentic, P. (2008). *Determinants of degree of leverage in Gulf Region States and Egypt,* Working paper, University of Montpellier.

All Africa Global Media. (2012). *Ibrahim Index of African Governance.* Retrieved from http://www.allafrica.com/stories/200905041508.html

Amartey-Vondee, E. (2007). Determination of life and health insurance premiums in Ghana; Practice, problems & prospects. Retrieved from *www.ssrn.com*

Amidu, M. (2007). Determinants of degree of leverage of banks in Ghana: An empirical approach, *Baltic Journal of Management,* 2 (1), 67-79.

Armstrong, M., & Baron, A. (2005). *Managing performance: Performance management in action* (2nd ed.) London: CIPD Publishing

Asimakopoulos, I., Samitas, A., & Papadogonas, T. (2009). Firm-specific and economy wide determinants of firm profitability: Greek evidence using panel data. *Managerial Finance,* 35 (11), 930 – 939

Baltagi, B.H. (2005). *Econometric analysis of panel data* (3rd ed.). Chichester: Wiley.

Barclay, M. J., & Clifford W. S. (2005). The degree of leverage puzzle: The evidence revisited. *Journal of Applied Corporate Finance,* 17, 8–17.

Berk, J., & DeMarzo, P. (2011). Corporate finance (2nd ed). Boston, Irwin McGrawHill.

Boachie-Mensah, F.O., & Marfo-Yiadom, E. (2010). *Strategic management,* Cape Coast. Nyakor Printing Works.

Brigham F. E., & Houston, F. J (2009). *Fundamentals of financial management* (9th ed). Boston, Mike Roche.

Bui, Y.N. (2009). *How to write a master's thesis,* U.K, Sage Publications International.

Caesar, G., & Holmes, S. (2003). Degree of leverage and financing of SMEs: Australian evidence. *Journal of Accounting and Finance,* 43 (3), 123-147.

Cheng, Y., Chien, C. & Liu, Y. (2010). Degree of leverage and firm value in China: A panel threshold regression analysis. *African Journal of Business Management.* 4 (12), 2500-2507.

Cooper, D.R., & Schindler P.S. (2001). *Business research methods.* Boston Irwin McGrawHill.

Desai, M. A., & Hines J. R. Jr. (2002). Expectations and expatriations: Tracing the causes and consequences of corporate inversions. *National Tax Journal*, 55 (2), 409-441.

Dhanasekaran, M., Kumar, A. M. S., Sandhya, S., & Saravanan, R. (2012). Determination of financial degree of leverage on the insurance sector firms in India. *European Journal of Social Sciences*, 29 (2), 288-294.

Dong, Z. (2011, July), *Foreign exchange rate and degree of leverage decision: A study of New Zealand listed property trusts.* Paper presented at the 17th Pacific Rim Real Estate Society Conference, Singapore. Retrieved from www.prresc.com.

Dreyer, J. (2010). *Degree of leverage: Profitability, earnings volatility and the probability of financial distress* (MBA dissertation, University of Pretoria, Pretoria, South Africa). Retrieved from http://upetd.up.ac.za/thesis/available/etd-04052011-120750/

El-Wahid, M. S. M., & Singapurwoko, A. (2011). The impact of financial leverage to profitability study of non – financial companies listed in Indonesia stock exchange. *European Journal of Economics, Finance and Administrative Sciences*, 32(3), 145-227.

Erol, M. (2011). Triangle relationship among firm size, degree of leverage choice and financial performance, some evidence from Turkey. *Journal of Management Research,* 11 (2), 87-98.

Esperança, J. P., & Mohamed. A. G. (2003). Corporate debt policy of small firms: An empirical (re)examination. *Journal of Small Business and Enterprise Development,* 4 (1), 1062–1080.

Fama, E. F., & French, K. R. (2005). Financing decisions: Who issues stock? *Journal of Financial Economics*, 76 (3), 549-582.

Frydenberg, S. (2004). *Theory of capital – A review.* Retrieved from http://ssrn.com/abstract=556631

Fu, A. C. (1997). *Relationship between degree of leverage and profitability: A time – series cross – sectional study on Malaysian*

Firms (Unpublished Master's Thesis) Universiti of Utara, Utara, Malaysia.

Gadzo, G. S & Gatsi. J. G. (2013). Firm level characteristics, macroeconomic factors and financial performance of insurance companies in Ghana. *International Journal for Business Administration and Management.* 3(1) 1-9.

Gadzo, G. S., Akoto, R. & Gatsi, J. G. (2014). Post-Merger Analysis of the Financial Performance of SG-SSB. *International Journal of Financial Economics, 3*(2), 80-91

Gadzo, S.G., Gatsi, J. G., & Oduro, R. (2016). Degree of Leverage and Risk Adjusted Performance of Listed Financial Institutions in Ghana. *Journal of Business and Management.* 18(1), 44-50

Gadzo, S.G., Gatsi, J. G., Anipa, A.A. & Ameyibor, J. (2016). Corporate Social Responsibility, Risk Factor and Financial Performance of Listed Firms in Ghana. *Journal of Applied Finance & Banking.* 6(2), 21-38

Gatsi, J. G., Gadzo, S. G. & Akoto, R. K. (2013). Degree of financial and operating leverage and profitability of insurance firms in Ghana. *International Journal of Business and Management, 7*(2), 57-65.

Gatsi, J. G., Gadzo, S.G., Okpoti, C. A. & Anipa, A.A. (2016). Determinants of market and book Based performance of manufacturing companies in Ghana: An empirical study. *International Journal of Economics, Commerce and Management* 4(1), 392-411

Gatsi, J.G, (2012). Degree of leverage of Ghanaian banks: An evaluation of its impact on performance. *IUP Journal of Bank Management,* 11 (4), 86-99.

Ghana Statistical Service Report (2011), *Annual Statistical Report.* Accra Ghana

Graf, F. (2010). *Risk adjusted profitability and degree of leverage of Banks-An empirical analysis* (Unpublished Dissertation). University of Konstanze.

Graham, J. (2000). How Big Are the Tax Benefits of Debt? *Journal of Finance,* 55 (3), 1901-1941

Graham, J.R. & Leary, M.T. (2010). *A review of empirical degree of leverage research and directions for the future*, Working paper Washington University St. Louis.

Gupta, S., & Newberry, K. (1997). Determinants of the variability in corporate effective tax rates: Evidence from longitudinal data. *Journal of Accounting and Public Policy*, 6, 16-34.

Hall, G. C., Hutchinson, P. J., & Michaelas, N. (2004). Determinants of the degree of leverages of European SMEs. *Journal of Business Finance and Accounting,* 31(6), 711-728.

Hausman, J. A. (1978). Specification tests in econometrics. *Econometrica*, 46 (6), 1251-1271.

Heinkel, R. (1982). A theory of degree of leverage relevance under imperfect information. *Journal of Finance*, 37, 1141-1150.

Heng, B. T., & Ong, T. S. (2011). Degree of leverage and corporate Performance of Malaysian construction sector. *International Journal of Humanities and Social Science*, 2 (1), 28-36

Im, K.S., Pesaran, M.H., & Shin, Y. (2003). Testing for unit roots in heterogeneous panels. *Journal of Econometrics,* 115 (1), 53-74.

Ishfaq, A., Naveed, A. & Zulfqar, A. (2010). Determinants of capital structure: A case of life insurance sector of Pakistan. *European Journal of Economics, Finance and Administrative Science*, 24 (1), 7-11.

Kaplan, S. R., & Norton, P.D. (1992). The balanced scorecard-measures that drive performance. *Harvard Business Review.* 23 (4),1-20.

Kayo, E.K. & Limura, H. (2010). Hierarchical determinants of degree of leverage. *Journal of Banking & Finance*, 35 (3), 358-371

Kim, H., Heshmati, A. & Aoun, D. (2006). Dynamics of degree of leverage: The case of Korean listed manufacturing companies. *Asian Economic Journal*, 20 (3), 275-302.

Lara, E. J., & Mesquita, C. M. J. (2002). Degree of leverage and profitability: The Brazilian case. *Center of postgraduate studies & research (CEPEAD),* The Federal University of the State of Minas Gerais (UFMG).

Levin, A., Lin, C.F., & Chu., C.S.J. (2002). Unit root test in panel data: Asymptotic and finite sample properties. *Journal of Econometrics*, 108, 1-24.

Levy, H., & Post, T. (2005). *Investments* (1st ed.), London: Prentice Hall.

Mahmud, M. (2003).The relationship between economic growth and degree of leverage of listed companies: Evidence of Japan, Malaysia and Pakistan, *The Pakistan Development Review,* 12 (2), 34-45.

Mazur, K. (2007). The determinants of degree of leverage choice: Evidence from Polish companies. *International Atlantic Economic Society*, 13 (2), 495-514.

Modigliani, F., & Miller, M. (1963). Corporate income taxes and the cost of capital: A correction. *American Economic Review*, 53 (2) 443-53

Murray, Z. F., & Vidhan, K. G. (2009). Profit and degree of leverage. *Journal of Finance,* 2 (1), 1 – 42.

Naizuli, R. W. (2011). *Degree of leverage and performance a case of selected medium sized enterprises in Kampala* (Unpublished master's Thesis). University of Makerere, Uganda.

Najjar, N., & Petrov, K. (2011). Degree of leverage of insurance companies in Bahrain. *International Journal of Business and Management,* 6, (11), 138 – 154

National Insurance Commission. (2017). *Annual report.* Accra.

Nivorozhkin, E. (2005). Degree of leverage in emerging stock market: The case of Hungry. *The Developing Economies*, 19 (2), 166–87.

Ooi, J. (1999). The determinants of degree of leverage: Evidence on UK property companies. *Journal of Property Investment & Finance*, 17 (5), 464-80.

Park,H. M. (2009). *Linear regression Model For panel data using SAS, STATA, LIMDEP and SPSS.* Indian University

Pratheepkanth, P. (2011). Degree of leverage and financial performance: Evidence from selected business companies in Colombo Stock Exchange Sri Lanka. *Journal of Arts, Science and Commerce*, 11 (1), 191-183.

Rajan, R.G., & Zingales, L. (2003). The great reversals: The politics of financial development in the 20th century. *Journal of Financial Economics*, 69 (1), 5–50.

Rauh, J.D., & Sufi, A. (2010), Degree of leverage and debt structure. *Review of Financial Studies,* 23 (2), 4242-4280.

Reimoo, Z. (2008). *Determinates of degree of leverage: Evidence from UK panel data* (Unpublished Master's Dissertation). University of Nottingham, UK.

Ross, S.A., Westerfied, R.W., Jeff, F.J., & Jordan, B. D. (2011). *Core principles and application of corporate Finance*. New York, McGraw-Hill/Irwin.

Saad, N. M. (2010). Corporate governance compliance and the effects to degree of leverage. *International Journal of Economics and Financial*, 2(1), 105-114.

Saunders, A., & Cornett, M.M. (2004). *Financial markets and institutions: A Modern Perspective* (2nd ed). Boston: McGraw-Hill,.

Sufian, F., & Muzafar, S. H. (2010). Does economic freedom foster Banks' performance? Panel evidence from Malaysia. *Journal of Contemporary Accounting and Economics*, 6 (1), 77 – 91.

Symeou, C. P. (2008). *The firm size – performance relationship: An empirical examination of the role of the firms growth potential* (Unpublished Master's thesis). University of Cambridge, United Kingdom.

Van-Horne, J.C., & Wachowicz. Jr. (2008). *Financial management.* England: Prentice Hall.

Watson, D., & Head, A. (2010). *Corporate finance principles and practice* (5th ed). London: Pearson Education Limited.

Westerlund, J., & Breitung, J. (2009). Myths and facts about panel unit root tests. *Mimeo, University of Gothenburb.*

Zikmund, W. (1997). *Business Research Method.* London: Cengage Learning.

APPENDICES

APPENDIX 'A' LIST OF COMPANIES USED FOR THE STUDY

Metropolitan Insurance Company Limited
Nsia Ghana Insurance Company Limited
Provident Insurance Company Limited
Quality Insurance Company Limited
Star Assurance Company Limited
Glico General Insurance Company Limited
Enterprise Insurance
SIC Insurance
Vanguard Assurance Company Limited
Ghana Union Assurance Company Limited
Phoenix Insurance Company Ghana Limited
Unique Insurance Company
Industrial And General Insurance Company (Ghana) Limited
Activa International Insurance Company Limited
Ghana Reinsurance
Mainstream Reinsurance
Colina Ghana Insurance Company Limited

APPENDIX "B" MEASUREMENT OF FIRM SPECIFIC ATTRIBUTES

Variables	Measurement
Return on Asset	$\frac{EBIT}{Total\ Assets} \times 100$
Return on Equity	ROA x Equity multiplier
Net Profit Margin	$\frac{EBIT}{Net\ Premium\ Income} \times 100$
Short-term Debt to Total Capital	$\frac{Total\ short\ term\ debt}{Total\ capital}$
Long term Debt to Total capital	$\frac{Total\ long\ term\ debt}{Total\ capital}$
Total Debt to Total Capital	$\frac{Total\ debt}{Total\ capital}$
Firm size	Log of total asset
Premium Growth	$\frac{Current\ Premium - Previous\ premium}{Previous\ premium}$
Age of firm	Year of Study – Date of establishment

www.ingramcontent.com/pod-product-compliance
Lightning Source LLC
Chambersburg PA
CBHW020434220526
45464CB00002B/692